Best
Pub Walks in
Cheshire
— Second Edition —

Jen Darling

SIGMA
Leisure

Published by Sigma Leisure – an imprint of:
Sigma Press, 5 Alton Road, Wilmslow, Cheshire, SK9 5DY, England.

British Library Cataloguing in Publication Data
A CIP record for this book is available from the British Library.

ISBN: 1-85058-755-8

Typesetting and Design by: Sigma Press, Wilmslow, Cheshire.

Cover photograph: The Pheasant Inn, Burwardsley

All other photographs by: Jen Darling except where indicated.

Printed by: Progress Press, Malta

Disclaimer: the information in this book is given in good faith and is believed to be correct at the time of publication. No responsibility is accepted by either the author or publisher for errors or omissions, or for any loss or injury howsoever caused. Only you can judge your own fitness, competence and experience.

Preface

'Best Pub Walks in Cheshire' contains thirty circular walks of varying lengths, all, except one, starting from a pub. In many of the walks other hostelries are mentioned *en route* – useful for those who can't stagger far without a halt for liquid refreshment(!), or others who wish to have a break half-way (perhaps for a pub lunch). Days when the pubs either do not open or don't serve meals, have been indicated, although these do alter from time to time, and it may be worth checking first. Apart from one or two notable exceptions, licensees do move around frequently, so, although the information is correct at the time of writing, if you particularly wish to sample a certain dish or beverage it is wise to check first. To help with this, the pub's telephone number is supplied where known.

Travelling instructions for each walk are given from the nearest large town. Most landlords are happy for ramblers to use the pub's car park provided they intend to call in for refreshment afterwards. However, wherever possible, and especially if the car park is small, the author has indicated an alternative parking place.

The length of each walk should be more accurate than in 'West Cheshire Walks' when a piece of cotton and a ruler were used! The author is finding a map measure an invaluable little gadget – provided she remembers to read off the distance in miles and not kilometres! In many of the walks there are short cuts back to the starting point for those with young children, others who have only a little time to spare – or for those of mature age for whom a short walk is preferable! There are no really high peaks in Cheshire, so none of the walks is as strenuous as those that scale the mountains of the Lake District.

The book is divided into six sections and, at the beginning of each, places worth visiting are mentioned. Thus, holiday-makers could combine days of walking with others sight-seeing – perhaps following a strenuous day with a more relaxing one. It is hoped that this information might also be an aid to locals when either planning a day out, or thinking up somewhere different to take the mother-in-law! The county's landscape varies considerably, from bleak, sheep-strewn slopes on the edge of the Pennines to the lush grasslands of the plain, and snippets about the local history of each area, as well as its fauna and flora, have also been included in the text.

The idea for 'Best Pub Walks in Cheshire' started as a bit of a joke while having a pub lunch with a friend. Collecting the information has been hard work but enjoyable, and the author is grateful to all the pub landlords who have taken the time and trouble to talk to her. She is well aware that many worthy Cheshire pubs are not mentioned and, depending on the success of the book, and the inclination of the publisher, she may, sometime in the future, contemplate writing a further volume. She would like to thank everyone who has given her information about their favourite pub and, if readers know others, she would be grateful to hear of them.

All ramblers in the county should be grateful to such bodies as Cheshire County Council for their maintenance of footpaths, stiles and bridges, to the Forestry Commission for providing walks over their land, and to the National Trust, who also preserve so much of our heritage. There are also local organisations, too numerous to name, whose aim is to preserve the countryside for future generations.

On a more personal basis, the author would like to thank both John Ellis from Cheshire Tourism and Joe Lawless of Camra, for their quotes on the back cover. A special thank you also goes to Valerie West for: initiating the idea, sampling pub grub on numerous occasions, and giving invaluable help with publicity. Thanks are also due to the author's husband for his rescue of both wife and caravan from a blizzard on the edge of the Pennines, and for spending much of his free time doggedly walking the routes – wife with notebook trotting resolutely behind.

Jen Darling

Contents

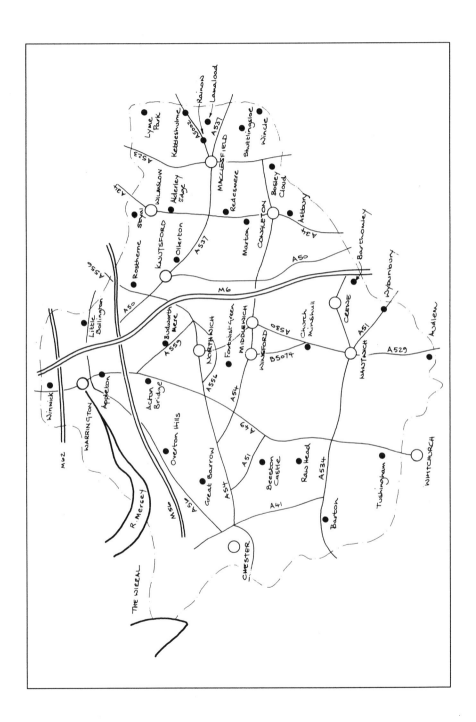

Key to Sketch Maps

`START`	Start of Walk
– – ▶ –	Route
– – – – –	footpath not on route
═══════	road
┬┬┬┬┬	canal
+-+-+-+	railway
∼∼○	river/lake
+	church
◊◊	woodland
⟁⟁	coniferous forest

All maps are to an approximate scale of 1:25 000

Introduction

Equipment

Little equipment is absolutely essential for walking in the Cheshire countryside. You shouldn't need crampons or even a compass unless you are really dedicated, and it is more comfortable to travel as uncluttered as possible. However, there are one or two basic necessities ...

A map The map reference is given at the start of both each section and each walk, and it's a good idea to have the relevant map with you. I have attempted to make the instructions as clear as posible but sometimes your interpretation may be different from mine - hopefully not often! The 1:25,000 maps are best but some walkers cope with the 1:50,000. It's up to you.

Footwear Boots are best, but wellingtons or trainers are possible. Cotton socks are preferable to nylon which cause blisters and, with boots, a pair of cotton socks with trousers tucked into a second woollen pair are ideal.

Clothes An anorak or cagoule is very necessary to cope with the vagaries of the British climate. A warm sweater, or two in the winter, is also a good idea; it is better to start off warm and then shed clothes. No-one minds what you look like in the country, so you can always sling a sweater round waist or shoulders if you get hot.

Miscellaneous A small rucksack is handy for oddments like plasters or a snack – apple, cheese or chocolate perhaps. Most back-packs have an extra pocket for loose change – in case you spot a likely place for liquid refreshment en route!

Walk this Way

'Best Pub Walks in Cheshire' has been written for anyone who enjoys combining a visit to an interesting local hostelry with a ramble through the county's varied countryside. Each pub has been visited and chosen for its distinctive history and character, its good food and drink, and its welcoming atmosphere. The walks are all based in Cheshire, the most southerly of the five counties comprising the North West of England. Some of the walks cover the bleak, sheep-strewn hillsides of the Pennines, others meander more gently over the patchwork plain, stride along the central sandstone ridge, or traverse the bumps and basins bordering Wales and Shropshire.

History

Cheshire's history dates back to early man. Significant finds include signs of Neolithic camps at Tatton Mere near Knutsford, the relics of a Bronze Age settlement at Winwick, 'Lindow Pete' so well preserved in the peat bogs near Wilmslow, and Iron Age forts like the one on Woodhouse Hill above Frodsham and Eddisbury Hill in Delamere Forest.

Roman settlements too are scattered around the county; Chester (Deva) was once an important fortress, its Roman amphitheatre the largest to survive in Britain. The discovery of salt near Northwich (Condate) and Middlewich (Salinae) also stems from that time, and there are several Roman roads which are still part of our road network today, such as Watling Street (now the A556) linking Chester with Manchester (Mamucium) and the A49 from Wigan passing through Winwick, Stretton, then running south to Whitchurch.

Many of Cheshire's towns and villages are mentioned in the Domesday Survey of 1066, including Great Budworth and Burwardsley, Wybunbury and Winwick, and several fortresses were built to withstand the continual threat of invasion by the Welsh, the most notable being Beeston Castle. Although Norman doorways, windows and stonework can still be found in many of our churches, for instance at Barthomley and Norton Priory, much of our early religious history stems from the Middle Ages, when religious houses like Vale Royal Abbey were founded. In the 16th century Armada beacons were established on high spots throughout the county, to provide early warning of a Spanish invasion, for instance, at Beeston Castle, on Beacon Hill above Frodsham, on Alderley Edge, and where White Nancy now stands on the Saddle of Kerridge. The county had a particularly troubled time during the Civil War years in the mid-17th century, the tiny hamlet of Barthomley being the scene of a savage and bloody massacre.

Between the 16th and 18th centuries the county was governed by its leading families of gentry, whose imposing mansions remain as a legacy for future generations. Examples of these are the Leghs of Lyme Park and Adlington Hall, and the Bromley-Davenports of Capesthorne.

In the 18th century, with the birth of the Industrial Revolution, workers flocked from field to factory. Samuel Greg's Quarry Bank Mill at Styal was one of the early pioneers of the cotton industry, shortly followed by others dotted all over the landscape at Bollington and Rainow, their chimneys and pools often still a stark reminder of a bygone age, while in Macclesfield the silk industry developed.

The Canal Age began at this time, followed by the Railway Era in the mid-19th century. Nowadays, Cheshire's network of footpaths and trails is varied enough to tempt any walker. Towpaths and obsolete railway lines provide many of these, with spectacular views from huge viaducts and aqueducts spanning deep valleys, like those at Bollington and North Rode.

Evidence of more recent industry can often by seen on the skyline. From Barrow Hill, Shell's Stanlow Oil Refinery swarms over the Mersey basin, while the massive cooling towers at Fiddlers Ferry and Ince show our dependency on electricity. At Winnington too the massive spread of ICI cannot be missed, and Daresbury's synchrotron tower signifies the importance of Nuclear Physics.

Farming

Clothed in wool to withstand the parky climate and sparse grass of the Pennine fields, sturdy sheep still cover many of the slopes in this area of the county. And to the west, the lush grass of the plain still proves ideal for dairy farming in a county renowned for its cheese, whether it be the crumbly red or white we know so well, or the more expensive Cheshire blue – orange and blue in colour, soft in texture and a worthy rival of Stilton.

With the decline in cattle-rearing, however, green meadows are sometimes now interspersed with yellow fields of rape, and tall crops of sweetcorn predominate near Beeston. Plant nurseries are also distributed prolifically throughout the region, from Little Bollington's growers of dahlias and chrysanthemums for the Manchester market, to fruit and vegetable growers, both large and small, on any sheltered slopes.

Leisure

Many of these walks are enhanced by the sight of other leisure-time activities – rock climbers splayed on the faces of Windgather Rocks and Helsby Hill, sailors on Redesmere and Budworth Mere, bird-watchers at Rostherne. Narrowboats and cruisers explore the network of canals, and fishermen can be found in innumerable spots on canal banks and beside reed-fringed pools, or at trout farms such as those at Marton and Wincle. Rights of way pass over several golf courses, the most hazardous perhaps being the one on the Astbury Walk. Immaculate bowling greens are tucked away in delightful village corners, and hockey, cricket or tennis can often be seen around Alderley and Appleton. Bridleways provide a soft surface for horse riding, while jumps set into hedges are used by the hunting fraternity, and a less welcome sight is the litter of spent discs from clay pigeon shooting near the Boar's Head (Wincle).

Pubs and Brewing

Many of the inns in the country districts of Cheshire were once farm-houses, where the farmer began to brew his own beer, selling it to farmhands and locals as a sideline. In this way the farmhouse parlour gradually became the community's social centre, and a village pub was born. In other places the pub developed as a place where industrial workers could slake their thirst after a hard day's work, miners from Poynton Colliery using the Miners' Arms, and the Kerridge quarrymen visiting the Redway Tavern. Other pubs have their roots in the canal era, Willeymoor Lock Tavern once being a lock keeper's cottage.

Although the 17th century saw the emergence of the professional brewer selling to other outlets, home brewing was still the general practice. Gradually, however, commercial brewers began to supply more pubs, and then bought them as tied houses until, in the last century, there were 60 commercial brewers in Cheshire alone. Unfortunately, with the big conglomerates buying up the smaller breweries, this number was reduced to five: Bass North at Preston Brook; the three Warrington breweries: Burtonwood, Greenall Whitley and Tetley-Walker; and the Oak Brewery at Ellesmere Port.

Many Cheshire pubs, however, belong to breweries operating from farther afield – Matthew Brown at Blackburn, Boddington's in Strangeways (Manchester), Higsons in Liverpool (now part of Boddington's), Marston's at Burton-on-Trent, Robinson's based in Stockport, and Webster & Wilson's in Halifax. And then there are the Free Houses who tend to stock a variety of beer from different breweries, a favourite being Ruddles County – from perhaps the most famous Real Ale brewery, based in Oakham.

It was totally accidental that none of the walks in this book is based on a Bass pub, but it is the only Cheshire-based brewery which produces no Real Ale. The battle for conversion continues. For the uninitiated, Real Ale is cask beer, where the barrel is tapped and the beer served through hand pumps at the bar. The alternative is gassy keg beer where carbon dioxide has been added – the beer is 'dead', the taste is bland, but the beer stays in a 'drinkable' condition for longer.

During the 20th century, country inns had to change to survive. The nooks and crannies of tiny smoke-shrouded rooms have largely disappeared. Sometimes the atmosphere has been lost too, in the conversion to one-room pubs, which are easier to clean and often have a dining area at one end. To compete with people drinking at home and in clubs many pubs now provide lunches and evening meals, and have added extra entertainment in the form of quiz nights and live music to the traditional darts and dominoes. Unfortunately, car parks have, in a few cases, obliterated bowling greens and gardens, but mostly these have survived, and children's play areas have been added to encourage family visits.

Conclusion

Much of Cheshire is covered by a plain of fertile pastures, meres and woodland, beribboned by rivers and canals, while market towns bustle with activity and even industry can look attractive from a distance. An irregular sandstone ridge runs down the centre and, on the eastern fringe, a belt of hills is shrouded with forest and heath.

This contrasting landscape makes Cheshire an attractive county for ramblers, 'magpie' cottages and sandstone churches dominating charming villages, where each local inn has its own inimitable feel and flavour. Whether they be nestling in a fold of the hills, enhancing a canal lock, or simply standing peacefully beside a country lane, all offer a warm welcome and good-value refreshment. What better way to explore this county, full of history and legend, interest and surprise, than on foot from a traditional English tavern.

North Cheshire

Acton Bridge	Mostly on Ellesmere Port (East) SJ47/57
Appleton	Warrington SJ 68/78
Budworth Mere	Northwich & Knutsford SJ67/77
Overton Hills	Ellesmere Port (East) SJ47/57
Winwick	Eccles (Greater Manchester) SJ69/79

There is plenty of variation in these five walks: experience ancient history around Winwick, enjoy extensive views over industrial Warrington and the Mersey estuary, savour Northwich's salt industry and the Anderton Boat Lift. When tired of walking, there are places to visit which should suit both old and young, serious-minded or frivolous and, included in this section are three quite different theme museums, all based on the area's past history.

Norton Priory

Norton Priory dates from as far back as 1134 when it was the home of Augustinian monks. A Norman doorway dating from 1180 still stands – the finest in Cheshire – and the prize-winning museum has the most comprehensive exhibition of medieval monastic life to be found in Britain.

It is surrounded by sixteen acres of woodland, where the excavated ruins and mosaic flooring of the Priory can still be seen and a pretty stream runs through a glade surrounded by banks of azaleas and rhododendrons. There is also a walled garden dating from the 18th century, plus laburnum arch and rose walk, herb garden, fruit arch and vegetable plot. Relics of the Tudor mansion and Georgian country house that were later built on the site can also be seen, and tile making, sculpture and carving take place regularly in craft workshops.

To reach Norton Priory, turn off the M56 at Junction 11 (A56) and head towards Warrington. Then follow the signs. It is open every afternoon between March and October. Telephone: Runcorn (01928) 569895.

Salt Museum

At present the Salt Museum can still be found beside the A533 in

Northwich; it is housed in Weaver Hall, once the workhouse for the area. However, plans are afoot to move it to the Lion Salt-works, Marston. Using a large variety of Visual Aids, enhanced by a tape and slide show, the Salt Museum tells the story of salt making in Cheshire from Roman times to the present day. It is open every afternoon except Monday throughout the year. Telephone: Northwich (01606) 41331.

Boat Museum

The Boat Museum at Ellesmere Port boasts the world's largest collection of traditional canal boats, many of which you can board to see how whole families lived and worked. There are also indoor exhibitions and a working pumphouse, and Porter's Row is a restored terrace of 1830s cottages. You can also take a trip along the Shropshire Union Canal or visit craft workshops on the site.

To reach the Boat Museum, leave the M53 at Junction 9 and follow the signs. It is open most days throughout the year. Telephone: Liverpool (0151) 355 5017.

Arley Hall and Gardens

This estate is still occupied by descendants of the original family – the Warburtons. The present brick-built hall dates from 1840, and was built by Rowland Egerton-Warburton. A colourful character and poet, his verses are still visible on signposts around the grounds. His artistic talents were passed down to his son who painted water colours, many of which can be seen in the house; and in the grounds is a private chapel designed by Anthony Salvin, where services are still held. Another building is a superb example of a cruck and timber tithe barn, probably dating from the late 14th century. A clock tower joins it to a Tudor barn, which once housed stables and has now been converted into a tea room. Nearby, a cabinet maker uses wood from the estate, and an artist creates fine bone chine figurines of Lewis Carroll's 'Alice' stories.

The gardens are impressive. The herbaceous border, dating from 1846, is thought to be one of the earliest established in England, and the avenue of cylindrical ilex is the only one of its kind anywhere. There is also an attractive avenue of pleached limes to saunter through, as well as banks of azaleas and rhododrendons, and gardens of roses and herbs, a scented garden, a vinery, a furlong walk, and several woodland paths.

Take the A559 towards Warrington from Northwich and turn right at Four Lanes Garage. Then follow the signs. Both hall and gardens are open everv afternoon except Monday between April and October. Telephone: Knutsford (01565) 777353.

For children, a pleasant innovation at Arley is a trailer ride to Stockley Farm, open three days a week. There they are encouraged to touch the animals, feed calves and lambs, or tumble about in the straw. Telephone: Knutsford (01565) 777323.

Risley Moss

We have the Warrington New Town Development Corporation to thank for opening up Risley Moss to the Public. It lies to the east of the town and is one of the last remaining areas of post-glacial mossland in the country. The Moss itself is the last remnant of the raised peat bog covered by sphagnum moss, which once covered the Mersey Valley from Warrington and Manchester in the north to Knutsford in the south. Much later, during the Industrial Revolution, farmers cleared the land and grew meagre crops, and the peat-cutting industry also thrived for a time, until the Second World War intervened and the whole area was left to decay.

In 1975 the Corporation decided to develop Risley Moss with three aims in mind – recreation for the people in the parkland, an education centre for school children and students to study both the social and natural history of the area, and conservation of the rare and fragile mossland. In 1980, David Bellamy performed the opening ceremony.

The Visitors' Centre is full of interesting displays and informative videos, and there are picnic sites, several woodland walks, two bird hides, and an observation tower which gives a grandstand view over the conserved mossland. And, on a clear day, one can pick out Croker Hill, Shutlingsloe, and other Pennine landmarks.

Take the A57 from Warrington, turning left alongside the Grange Industrial Estate before you reach the M6. At the seventh roundabout turn right along Birchwood Way, then right again down Moss Gate which leads to the main entrance. Risley Moss is open on most days. Telephone: Warrington (01925) 824339.

Walton Hall Gardens

Walton Hall Gardens extends over fifty acres of parkland on the outskirts of Warrington, with spectacular displays of azaleas and rhododendrons in May. There is also a bowling green, putting and crazy golf, a pets' corner and a children's old-fashioned playground, with swings, slides, roundabouts and see-saws. The two advantages of a visit to Walton Park on the southern outskirts of Warrington are that it is always both open and free!

Marbury Country Park

Marbury Country Park on the outskirts of Northwich is skirted on the walk around Budworth Mere. Deciduous woodland surrounds 190 acres of parkland on the banks of this pretty mere, and there are several walks to follow, whilst naturalists and bird watchers can enjoy the abundant wildlife.

Take the A533 north-west from Northwich, turn right to Anderton and continue until you reach the park's entrance on your right. There is a small charge for parking. Telephone: Northwich (01606) 77741.

All the fun of the fair at Pickmere

Save up your 2p pieces for a visit to Pickmere, then gamble them away on old-fashioned one-arm bandits – the ones with the row of cherries! Dodgems, swingboats and a roundabout provide further amusement, together with boating on the lake.

Take the A599 north from Northwich. Turn right to Pickmere and follow the signs.

Thrills and chills on the Ghost Train at Pickmere

Acton Bridge

Route: Trent and Mersey Canal – River Weaver – Dutton Locks – Cliff Lane – Acton Cliff – Crowton – Acton Brook – Acton Bridge – A49

Distance: 6 miles

Start: Leigh Arms (SJ 602760)

By Car: Take the A49 south from Warrington for several miles, crossing over the M56 and then passing a Little Chef at the junction with the A533. The Leigh Arms is set back on the left as you reach the swing bridge over the River Weaver.

The Leigh Arms – 01606 853327 (Burtonwood)

Dating from the 16th century the Leigh Arms was once a coaching inn on the busy A49, which used to pass the front door and, opposite, the old brick bridge over the Weaver can still be seen. The stable block has disappeared, but at one time the gentry, having stabled their horses, would book a room and a serving wench for the night, and the room numbers can still be seen behind the bar.

The small, cosy rooms have disappeared and the pub has been extended with new kitchens, but the wooden beams and many of the furnishings are still original, and there is some wonderful stained glass, including one panel behind the bar of the Cheshire hunt. Fat Thomas Forshaw is portrayed in a stained glass window advertising Threlfalls', and another jovial character promotes Silver Buckle Ale, both also being depicted in panelling and pictures. On the walls are local scenes of the pub and the Weaver, and one showing the lock gates at Dutton.

The Leigh Arms has always been a Burtonwood pub, and still serves hand-pulled traditional Real Ale from its old-fashioned pumps. Notice the stained glass as you go through the front door, and enter what was once the tap room. Ahead are the original stained glass doors over the bar. Surprisingly, and unlike almost every other Cheshire pub, there seems to be no authentic ghost at all. But, for many years, old Harry Trevor (owner of the furniture removal company) used to walk in on a Sunday, announcing in a loud voice, "Ah've just come to see how th' ghost's doing. He often meets me here on Sunday." No-one else ever emptied the pub quite so quickly!

A full range of meals is served both at lunchtime and in the evening, and there is always a traditional Sunday lunch laid on each week. Parties of up to forty can be catered for in the back room, and walkers are always wel-

Once a busy coaching inn – the Leigh Arms at Acton Bridge

come. Outside, a pleasant garden borders the river for warmer days, and there is a play area for children.

In the summer trips down the River Weaver in The Princess start from here, and parties can book for a whole day's outing with lunch. The boat also sails to Northwich on Market Day (leaving at 10.30am) for people who wish to go shopping there, and on Sundays pleasure trips take place, often with live entertainment.

The Walk

As you leave the car park, cross the road to the apex of a road triangle where you will see, beside the gate to The Paddock, a footpath sign almost hidden behind a fir bush. To reach the Trent-and-Mersey Canal, go down this path and over a stile. Then walk along the side of a field to a further stile, after which you climb through a coppice and turn left along the towpath.

There is a steady rumble of traffic as the canal narrows to pass under the A49, and then you pass the firm advertising Black Prince Holidays, their boats brightening the bank with splashes of red and green, blue and yellow. Leave the towpath at the next bridge (210) and cross over it to follow a bridleway across a rough field. Cinders have been thoughtfully laid in the muddiest places. Bear left at the end of this – where the sign indicates – and walk along the hedge parallel with the canal. The long ridge of the Overton Hills stretches along the skyline, ending abruptly in a sheer scarp.

When you reach a copse drop down through it. In autumn you pass between mounds of soggy, blackened bracken, before bearing right to leave the wood and walk round the field. Leave this through the gate, turning left down a farm track to cross the canal bridge before continuing down a wide track to the River Weaver. Cross the rusted iron stile here and turn right, perhaps passing a dredger deepening the river bed. It used to be a much busier waterway than it is today, when barges and sea-going vessels carried salt from Winsford to Liverpool, and then on to other parts of the world.

When you arrive at the white bridge, where the river has been considerably straightened, continue along the towpath to Dutton Locks. Here, after crossing the river, follow the footpath sign away from the water with the trees on your right. Then, as you enter a field, keep the hedge on your left and the hill on your right as you walk to a facing stile, where you turn right along the muddy cart track to Manor Farm. A large, mossy boulder gives you a leg up into the farmyard, out of which you exit over another stone.

Keep ahead along Cliff Lane, which leads past Willow Cottage to Weaver Holt and, when you come to the T-junction, turn right; the country lane then drops down under the railway. After this you turn left down a cart-track, and bear right up the hill to pass an orchard of low-growing apple trees before climbing over a stile at the track's end.

This area is known as Acton Cliff and, as you follow the path's line across the field, you have a good view of the many arches of Dutton viaduct as it carries the railway high above the Weaver. Care is needed where the path can be treacherous as it drops steeply down to Cliff Brook. Cross the bridge here and climb over the stile ahead to walk over marshy ground. Then keep left over Dane's Gutter; after which the soft, sandy soil is pock-marked with rabbit holes as the line of alder and oak indicates the way to a gate, where you exit to the road and Poplar Farm.

Turn left, passing Yew Tree Farm and, when the road bears right, you turn left again and climb a stile into the right-hand field. Walk down this meadow to cross Crowton Brook, and then continue alongside Acton Brook until you cross a stile. Turn away from the brook here, and keep alongside the hedge until you reach the road. Crowton village is over to your right but you turn your back on it to pass Ivy House and then Birch House.

Watch out for the left turn down a pot-holed road (signposted Acton Bridge) where the massive bulk of Frodsham Hill is clearly visible as you walk between two neatly clipped hawthorn hedges to reach Acton Brook

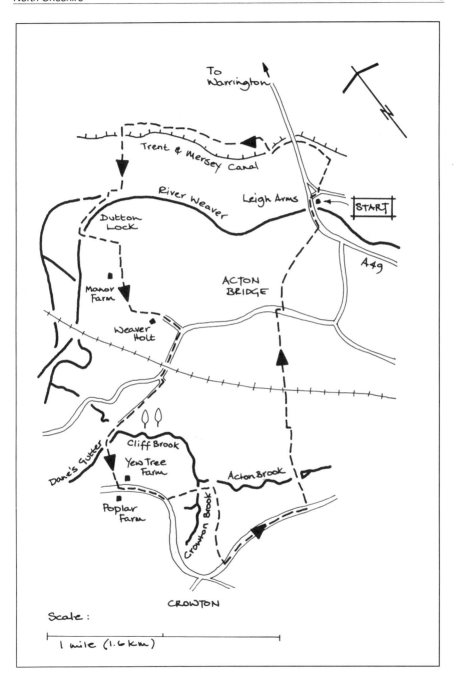

once more. It has been artificially widened here to make a large, pleasant pool, out of which the water overflows noisily on its way to the Weaver.

Keep on past a clump of bamboo to where a yellow arrow shows the way over two stiles, the second leading to a field perhaps occupied by a donkey. Carry on down the field's side, turning left over the stile in the corner. Then head for a telegraph pole, a tree, and a hedge's end, before turning right alongside the latter.

You soon reach the busy railway line and cross it with care. It is a main line and trains are frequent. Carry straight ahead across the long field in front of you, the way stretching out like a narrow ribbon as the houses of Acton Bridge village come into view. Finally, cross a stile between two gates and keep ahead again to a further stile, from which a grassy track drops down to the road.

Turn right and immediately left between a house and a bungalow; climb over a stile and then drop down the field ahead. Here you may see rabbits romping in the sandy soil of the steep bank, and journey's end is in sight. To get there, cut across the marshy ground to the far right-hand corner where there is a sturdy bridge over a stream. Then keep the hedge on your left until it cuts away, and you go ahead over a dyke and through any of the large gaps in the hedge. After this, make for an iron stile in the facing hedge, from which steps lead up to the A49. (You will probably be glad to leave this low lying marshland which can be extremely wet and boggy.) Turn left along the main road, crossing the bridge, one of the oldest electric swing bridges in the world, to arrive back at the Leigh Arms.

Appleton

Route: Stretton – Hatton Lane – Hill Cliffe – Rabbit Run – Birchdale Road – London Bridge – Bridgewater Canal – The Dingle – Ford's Rough – Cann Lane – Pewterspeare – Cat and Lion

Distance: 7.5 miles

Start: Cat and Lion car park (SJ 618827)

By Car: Take the A49 from Warrington and continue through Stockton Heath and Appleton. After passing Warrington Golf Club keep ahead at a round-about; then turn right at Stretton traffic lights to park behind the Cat and Lion.

This is an invigorating and varied walk with glorious views over Warrington and the Mersey Valley; a handy chocolate bar from Stretton Newsagents could increase your stamina as you set off at a spanking pace along Hatton Lane. Climb over the stile opposite houses dating from 1936 and continue down the field ahead, where the panoramic view of industrial Merseyside contrasts sharply with the rich, rolled greens of Warrington Golf Course. The controversial, concrete tower of Daresbury Nuclear Physics Laboratory soon adds a further dimension as you cross the stile.

Turn right, walking round two sides of the next field to reach another stile, and then continue ahead until, about halfway down the hedge, you cross a ditch and stile into another field. Go over this to a stile and then proceed along a cart-track until you turn right to Stockton Heath. The line of the path is clearly visible as it crosses the middle of the next two fields and then skirts to the right of a small coppice of tree-fringed pools.

Keep ahead with the hedge first on your left and then on your right to a bracken-fringed field path bordering a tiny stream which is soon crossed. As the brick-strewn track alternately widens and narrows, the lion-guarded monument – once a folly on the Lyons family estate – is visible atop the highest point of the area.

You soon turn left at the T-junction towards Appleton Reservoir along a wide track, leaving it for a narrow path between ponds which then crosses a field. The windows of Bellfields Farm glintingly catch the light as you cross the stile onto Firs Lane. Turn right uphill (ignoring the Delamere Way footpath ahead) then take the next left turn along the footpath to Hillcliffe.

Here, the view stretches before you like the unrolling of a magnificent mural – Daresbury tower, Appleton Reservoir, Frodsham and Helsby Hills; the Mersey curving under Runcorn Bridge to Fiddlers Ferry, while the pastoral landscape surrounding Walton Hall and church is backed by Bold Colliery and the diverse industrial scene of Warrington - the whole panorama a glorious miscellany of old and new, man-made and natural.

Keep ahead along here to the ancient burial ground of Hill Cliffe. Then, briefly turn left down Red Lane at the prominent black and white lychgate before crossing into Highwood Road. Turn left again down a beech-bordered snicket, its sandstone path and rough hewn steps known locally as the Rabbit Run, where the older generation have seen the antics of rabbits on these once-grassy slopes replaced by children's imaginative games.

Bear right at Delphfields Road, and then left to continue down beside another beech hedge until, after crossing the junction of Kingsley Drive and Warren Drive, you reach Birchdale Road and turn right. The London Bridge pub is soon in view with its whitewashed walls and bright blue paintwork.

London Bridge – 01925 267904 (Scottish & Newcastle)

This pub originates from the late 18th century when the Bridgewater Canal was completed from Manchester as far as this point, and the area became known as Stockton Quay. Coal from the mines at Worsley was shipped down the canal to be distributed to the neighbouring communities, and farmers sent potatoes back, to be marketed in Manchester.

Stockton House, the large dwelling opposite, was once occupied by the agent in charge of the wharf and his family, while the building adjoining the pub used to be the smithy, and a brickmaker's crane used to stand on the patio. Here too is the rounded flight of steps where people once boarded passenger boats to Manchester when the fare was 1d a mile. The service, which only ended in 1918, was the last to become obsolete in England, and the boat, the *Duchess Countess*, had an S-shaped knife on her bow which was used to slice ruthlessly through any obstructions.

At the pub the ghost of a former licensee, Jack Green, who hanged himself in the mineral store when his wife absconded with another man, is said to haunt the building.

Children are welcome in a room away from the bar, and the varied menu includes several homemade dishes.

Walk continued ...

As you cross London Bridge and drop down onto the tow-path brightly-coloured pleasure boats offer a reminder of the popular rally which takes place each July when canal barges arrive from all over the country. The cantilever bridge soon appears, standing high above the Manchester Ship Canal, and the spire of Warrington parish church soars behind – third tallest in the

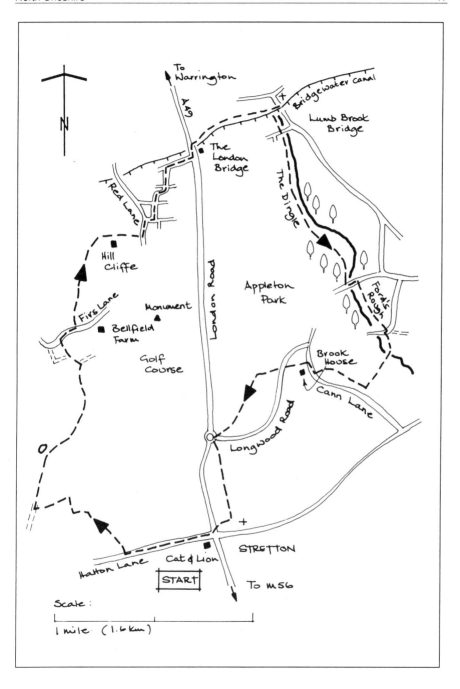

country – while steam billows into the icy air from the chimneys of Crosfield's soap factory.

Leave the towpath by doubling back after crossing Lumb Brook Bridge – an aqueduct built by the famous engineer, Brindley. A record of road repairs pertaining to it in an ancient ledger reads, '1737. Repairing Bridge at Lumb Brook 3s'. You wouldn't get much work done for three shillings (15p) nowadays! A more recent structure here is Bethesda Chapel, opened in 1957 after part of the canal bank had been carved away to take the foundations.

Go under the bridge and continue down a rough slip-road in front of some houses before crossing Bridge Lane and keeping along a grassy track. Lumb Brook burbles beside you as you pass the ends of Wood Lane and Hinton Crescent, and then continue along a litter-strewn footpath into the pleasanter reaches of 'The Dingle', with its banks of evergreen rhododendrons, deciduous trees and varied wild life.

Turn left when you reach Dingle Lane and then immediately right after crossing the stream, into Fords Rough. Much work has been done recently to make the path here less hazardous, and this stretch is a very pretty part of the walk, the stream sparkling below and, in Spring, colourful clumps of bluebell and primrose spangle the slopes.

Climb over the stile out of this miniature valley and turn right into Green Lane – the dulcet tones of Appleton Thorn footballers perhaps resounding in the chilly air! Ignore the bridleway that goes to the left as you cross the stile into a field, and walk up the hedge to cross a further stile, this time on your right. Keep ahead for a short distance before veering left to pass between an electricity post and the tree that marks the end of an obsolete hedge. Turn right at the oak tree in the facing hedge which leads you over a stile into a newly planted copse of oak, holly, beech and fir. When you come to a path turn right, dropping down steps to cross the bridge over Dipping Brook before turning left along a path – its gravelled surface maybe catching the sun's rays like a host of silicon chips.

Turn right up Cann Lane, passing Brook House as it broods disapprovingly over the building developments disrupting the once rural scene. Then turn left down a bridleway where trees, shrubs and reeds form an effective and delicate mirror in the shimmering water of a pond. You soon cross winding Longwood Road and keep left down the bridleway as it runs parallel with Pewterspeare Lane to a roundabout.

Cross over here and continue along the footpath (past the statue of the two-faced Roman god, Janus) to Stretton Church, the area behind it recently preserved from property developers, and now being attractively landscaped for local use. The path goes to the right of the hawthorn hedge

St Matthew's Church, Stretton

(past more Roman statues) and on to the vicarage, where the ancient Roman road from Warrington to Northwich once ran through the garden.

Journey's end is in sight but you may wish to pause at the church. The clock on the tower is of particular interest, being one of only two in the country where lettering replaces numerals. 'Time is not all' and 'Forget not God' are golden words in golden paint on the west and south walls. There is a lych gate erected by the Lyons family who lived at Appleton Hall, and the beautiful stained glass window at the east end of the chancel is dedicated to the memory of a much-loved vicar – Canon Cross. He died in 1937 but is still remembered with affection by older parishioners.

For physical refreshment, walk along the tarmac path behind the Vicarage to the Cat and Lion and, if you happen to arrive in the afternoon after closing time, hot pies and other goodies can be purchased from the Beehive Stores.

The Cat and Lion – 01925 730451 (Scottish & Newcastle)

The Cat and Lion was built at the beginning of the 18th century by the Lyons family, who had close connections with Greenalls, the brewers,and whose coat of arms incorporated a Cheshire cat. Hence the origin of the inn sign and the rhyme that encircles it – *'The lion is strong and the cat is vicious, My ale is strong and so are my liquors.'*

This pub has always had a warm and friendly atmosphere but since its refurbishment it has also gained a reputation for good food. Besides the dishes advertised in its Miller's Kitchen menu, it also produces a varied selection of 'specials' each day to suit all pockets and palates. From full meals to home-made soup or a sandwich.

Budworth Mere

Route: Cock o'Budworth – Great Budworth – Marston – Trent and Mersey Canal – Anderton Lift – Budworth Mere

Distance: 7 miles

Start: Cock o' Budworth (SJ 657778)

By Car: Take the A49 from Warrington. When you reach the M56 round-about take the A559 to Northwich, and don't be tempted to stop as you pass the Ring o' Bells, the Birch and Bottle and the Antrobus Arms en route for the Cock. It is on the right as you approach the left turn to Great Budworth.

Cock o' Budworth – 01606 891287 (Joseph Holt)

As with so many Cheshire pubs the Cock was once a farm, and the first person to run it as a pub was a woman. By 1735, when the front part was added, it had become a coaching inn. The restaurant was converted from the shippon and cowsheds, the spacious conservatory is a no smoking area, and the upper storey now forms a function room where, with prior notice, meetings can be held.

The Cock was the first headquarters for Budworth Sailing Club before its clubhouse was built on the shores of the mere. Children can eat in the back room and there is an adventure playground outside together with a football pitch. Walkers are always welcome in this friendly and interesting pub.

The Cock is often associated with Drunken Barnaby, a roguish poet who stayed in 1643 on his way home from Warrington. His rhymes can be seen on the wall,

'Thence to th' Cock o' Budworth, where I drink strong ale as brown as berry, 'til at last with deep healths felled, to my bed I was compelled.'

or

'Came to Cock o' Budworth where I drank strong ale as brown as berry. I for state was bravely sorted, by two porters well supported.'

Unfortunately, he must have overdone the 'strong ale' on his final visit, for he was thrown out for drunkenness, and was killed on his way home. His body was brought back to the pub to rest, and since then strange happenings have been attributed to his ghost – articles inexplicably moved, the refusal of the landlord's dogs to enter one of the rooms.

The Walk

This is an interesting walk. Outstanding landmarks are never far out of sight – the battlemented tower of Great Budworth Church, the Anderton Boat Lift, or the vast ICI complex at Winnington. When the skyline is filled by the mass of this industry it is easy to see how Northwich became known as 'The Black Country of the North'. Dr. Ludwig Mond founded ICI and his statue stands amid the huge chemical works lining the river.

Although parts of the route can be muddy, it passes near so many different kinds of water, including meres, salt flashes, rivers and canals, that it is well worth putting up with the resulting filthy boots or muddy wellies!

Leave the car park and turn left uphill along the A559. Then go right down Belmont Road at Fairfield Cottage – its cruck beams clearly visible in its bulging side wall. You soon pass the entrance to Cransley School and see Budworth Church peeping out above trees.

Where the road goes off to Antrobus and Warrington notice the house on the corner, cleverly converted from a school. It dates from 1845 and still has its sturdy, studded oak door. Opposite this road is a grassy track, leaf-strewn in Autumn, down which you turn, passing through an iron kissing gate at the end and keeping to the right of the next field.

The village of Great Budworth stands out ahead, dominated by the towering bulk of its church and tower. It once used to be the centre of a huge parish which stretched from the Mersey, near Warrington, to Holmes Chapel in the south-east. Its church, made of local stone, is a prominent landmark, and has been described as, 'a church that sits on a knoll with cottages clustered around it like a hen with her chicks'.

Cross the stile and keep right again. The electricity pylons march across the landscape here, their cables sizzling overhead, a collecting point for migrating birds. Climb over the stepladder into the next field and turn left down the hedge of hawthorn interwoven with brambles. Then walk round the end of this field to a stile by the gate. Keep ahead down the next field towards the church, and climb the stile at the end.

The mellow chimes of the church clock may ring out the time as you turn left along the track into the village – described by Arthur Mee as 'a rare bit of Tudor England'. You soon pass the old village hall and the newer bowling green and tennis court. Modern houses give way to cottages of old world charm, their names often denoting their original use – The Old Smithy, Smithy Cottage, Hough Farm, Ring o' Bells.

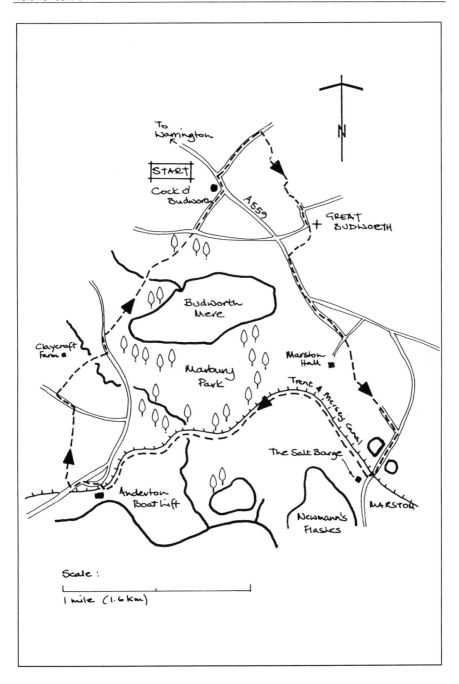

St. Mary and All Saints, Great Budworth

This massive 16th century church of perpendicular design has a crenellated tower which houses eight bells – once a difficult ring with a delightful sound. As is true of many towers, this one tended to move as the bells were rung, and an elderly ringer tells of the time a man's jacket disappeared through a crack in the wall while he was ringing for a wedding! The ringers had to continue until the crack opened up again and the coat could be extricated! The bells have now been rehung – a great improvement.

Inside the church are medieval stalls and unusual carvings, and a beautiful stained glass window of the manger scene. Designed by Kempe, it contrasts the kings' costly presents with the adoration of the humble shepherds, one wearing a patched coat, another playing bagpipes.

On the north side of the churchyard stands the old schoolhouse. Built in Shakespeare's time, stone foundations support brick walls, lightened by tiny mullioned windows, and topped by a gabled roof. Opposite, on School Lane, are the oldest houses in the village. Timber-framed with brick infill, they date from the 17th century.

Opposite the lychgate stands the George Inn, built in 1722, its studded oak door topped by a massive stone lintel two feet thick. It too was once a coaching inn, and nowadays is worth a visit, with appetising food and Real Ale. Outside is the old well, its canopy intact and, by the churchyard wall, the village stocks still stand.

Continue down South Bank, between modern vicarage and ancient church, and turn right at the end. You then bear left in front of a bungalow to a wide grassy track, where the view opens out over Marston and the flat, mirror-like sheen of Budworth Mere. The name Great Budworth actually means 'dwelling by the water' which seems most appropriate when standing here. Behind the mere ICI forms an industrial backdrop to the rural scene as you keep along the field hedge until the path very obviously drops down to the road.

Opposite is the entrance to Budworth Sailing Club, the masted boats lurching at haphazard angles round the clubhouse as you turn left to walk down the road to a sweeping bend. Keep ahead over a stile here and the path stays parallel to the road behind a row of houses. At another stile you cross a lane and a further stile into a field.

The next part of the walk may be churned up by cows as you go down a grassy field, keeping the barbed wire on your right, until you cross a stile followed by a stepladder. You then follow another barbed wire fence across a field with bright yellow arrows clearly defining the route along the sides of the remaining fields. Marston Hall is nearby and you get a glimpse of the Trent and Mersey Canal as it emerges from Marbury Woods. As you reach

Cottages of ancient charm in Great Budworth village

the road at Harris's, turn right to continue between two 'flashes' – the end product of subsidence caused by pumping out salt brine from beneath the surface. Bullrushes fringe the banks and these wild areas are the haunts of swans, ducks, coots – and anglers!

Ahead is the village of Marston, with a switchback street and cottages lying at drunken angles – again caused by land subsidence from salt mining. This whole area is built on pillars of salt which are slowly dissolving, whole houses tumbling without warning into the old brine pits. Here, the Old Mine was one of the biggest in England. 360 feet deep and covering 35 acres, it was visited by the Tsar of Russia in 1844 when he dined inside by the light from 10,000 lamps. Open to the public for a time, 1,000 people are said to have visited it in a day.

Cross the bridge. The Lion Salt Works to your left was the last place in the area to stop producing salt by the 'open pan' method. At present it serves as a ghostly reminder that the prosperity of Northwich has always been based on salt. In fact, the area still accounts for two-thirds of the salt brine produced in this country, and a heritage centre for the industry is now being created here.

Ahead is the local pub, aptly named The Salt Barge. You may wish to warm your cockles here before turning right to face the wind that nips along the canal bank. Walk along the towpath. Newman's Flashes, to your left, is the largest of the salt lakes, and you may catch a glimpse of Witton Church – the oldest building in Northwich – its roof originating from Norton Priory.

Before reaching the southern boundary of Marbury Park you pass one of the distinctive panda-like iron signposts, peculiar to the Trent and Mersey Canal, and which, along this stretch, indicate the mileage between Preston Brook and Shardlow. As you reach the trees you may be lucky enough to spot a red squirrel scampering about; and don't miss the mighty beech, its branches spread wide to keep the other trees at bay, its pock-marked trunk covered in green algae.

Marbury Country Park may be glimpsed through the trees and is well worth a visit for bird watching or other natural pursuits! It abounds with interest and legend, and the hall, now razed to the ground, is still reputed to have a ghost - the white lady.

As you pass the cottage called Jackson's Turn notice the sturdy iron rings set in concrete where boats can be moored. Then cross the bridge that goes over the cut to Clare Cruisers before continuing along the towpath to Anderton Marina, with its large variety of brightly-coloured boats for hire. Vessels are moored along the opposite bank from here until you reach a sheltered picnic spot, which provides a good view of the Anderton Lift, and a close-up of the ICI works at Winnington.

The Anderton Boat Lift is one of the Wonders of Cheshire. This incredible construction was the first of its kind in the world and is the only remaining one in Britain. Its purpose is to raise and lower boats 50 feet 4 inches between the Trent and Mersey Canal and the River Weaver. The lift, which takes five minutes per journey, replaced a system of locks which used to take one-and-a-half hours. It was first opened in 1875 when it was operated by a hydraulic mechanism, this being converted to electricity in 1907. The lift was shut down by British Waterways in August 1983 due to the corrosion of the main support legs. There have been vociferous protests about its prolonged closure and the Friends of the Anderton Boat Lift has been formed; it is hoped that the structure will eventually be back in operation.

Turn right over the footbridge and then left to walk to the village of Anderton down Old Road, passing the Stanley Arms and Walkers coach firm. (When you reach the main road there is also a well-stocked village shop a few yards to your right where you can buy snacks.) However, you turn left and then immediately right down a track, along which you soon turn right again over a stile into a field. Bear diagonally left over this field to another stile in a barbed wire fence, and then continue ahead over another stile. Keeping the field boundary on your left, continue to a further stile in a facing hedge, after which you cross the field ahead to the road and turn left.

The Anderton Boat Lift *(photo: Graham Beech)*

Along here you soon turn right over a stile into a field, across which the footpath is clearly defined to a stile at the side of the gate ahead. Claycroft Farm is over to your left as you keep forward to a stile which takes you into the wood ahead, through which you pass, crossing a sturdy bridge, its ornate railing providing both interest and safety. As you exit from here you have a hawthorn hedge for company until you turn left at the road.

Go immediately right through a small wooden gate in the hedge to cross the field to a stile, after which you keep forward, with a barbed wire fence on your left, down to a footbridge over a stream. Cross this and walk beside the fence to cross the next field on higher ground, and with luck the sun will be sparkling on the glassy surface of Budworth Mere. It was used as a fish hatchery in the Middle Ages, and even now is well stocked with bream and pike, while reed warblers and great crested grebes breed in its reeds. Marbury Hall once stood in the parkland, a stately home which offered shelter to Polish refugees in the Second World War.

Leave the fence when you spot the footpath into the copse ahead and walk between towering beeches to the road. Continue up the road ahead past Sandicroft and you will soon have come full circle back to The Cock.

The Overton Hills

Route: The Ridgeway — Woodhouse Hill Fort — Mickledale — Riley Bank — Alvanley Cliff — Simmond's Hill — Alvanley

Distance: 7 miles

Start: The White Lion (SJ 497740)

By Car: Take the A56 east from Chester. As you approach the outskirts of Helsby turn right to Alvanley. Then turn right again on the outskirts of the village, and park at the White Lion.

White Lion – 01928 722949 (Scottish & Newcastle)

The pretty village of Alvanley grew up as a farming community and the white-fronted pub was built around 1700 as a farmhouse. The milk parlour stands behind as a separate building, the landlord once combining a milk round with the job of licensee. The surrounding area, composed of hill, field and woodland, traversed by a network of footpaths, makes ideal walking country and, although there isn't a separate room for ramblers at this

The White Lion at Alvanley

friendly pub, they are always welcome – a long line of muddy boots often on parade at the door.

The White Lion has well deserved its triumphs as regional winner of the Pubs in Bloom competition, and the licensee has also been voted Innkeeper of the Year for the Chester area from time to time. There is now a patio, beer garden and a non-smoking area inside.

Food is served at lunchtime and in the evenings seven days a week, and all day on Sundays. The many 'specials' usually include three meats plus other dishes such as home-made chicken and mushroom pie, chicken chasseur and lasagne. The home-made hot pot and cottage pie is probably the best value-for-money meal in Cheshire. Bar snacks are also available, together with a mouth-watering sweet trolley.

The Walk

Cross to where the diminutive spire tops the village church. Here, a unique custom called 'roping' once forced newly-married couples to pay a mone-tary forfeit before leaving the lychgate, which would then be used by locals to toast the happy couple in the pub opposite!

Walk to the Georgian building of Church House Farm which faces your left turn alongside Rose Cottage. Walk beside its garden, then continue up the long field and climb over a stile almost opposite the idyllic setting of Alvanley Cricket Club. Continue in the same direction but on the other side of the hedge, climbing two more stiles before dropping down to an area between ponds, and clambering over a stone-pillared, sturdy stile onto the road.

Bear slightly left before following a footpath down the edge of a field. The scarp slopes of the Overton Hills frame the industry of the Mersey Valley ahead. Beside you clumps of spiky reeds line a waterless, v-shaped valley. At the end of the field cross a stile and follow the hedge round to the left, the right-of-way skirting a small copse to the holly hedge ahead. Walk along-side this and turn right in front of the bridge to walk (muddy patches per-mitting) beside the stream to the road.

Here, turn left down Burrows Lane. The look-out post on Foxhill Wood is prominent ahead as you go right at the T-junction and continue up the hill along the ancient hill-crossing route known as The Ridgeway. Just before the entrance to a caravan site, turn left along the Sandstone Trail, which you now follow all the way to the bottom of Abrahams's Leap. (There is just one junction on this part of the route and, in case the sign is missing, you turn left.) Along here the broad track shelters below the brow of the hill, sandy banks providing ideal homes for rabbit, fox and badger, while swathes of bracken and rhododendron sprawl up the hillside.

Eventually you reach Woodhouse Hill Fort – one of seven Iron Age forts along the sandstone ridge of West Cheshire. Only an earth mound remains, but ancient families would have lived here in huts. Sheltered from the weather by the tree-covered hillside, the summit would have provided a vantage point from which to spot sudden danger. It does not matter which way round this hill you walk as the paths join up at the far side and continue to a fine viewpoint from a sandstone slab – a delightful picnic spot.

As you continue along the top of the hill, to your left the small town of Helsby comes into view. Nestling under the sphinx-like profile of its hill, the drained marshland below is now used for agriculture. The folk who live hereabouts use Helsby Hill as a weather indicator, and there is a local saying, 'As long as Helsby wears a hood, the weather's never very good!'

Clamber down huge sandstone steps formed from weathered rock, known locally as Abraham's Leap. You actually turn right here leaving the Trail but, if you first fancy a little more climbing, ahead is Jacob's Ladder – a further challenge, although there is now a path round this obstacle for the less ambitious.

Retrace your steps if you have made this detour and turn left over a stile. Keep ahead over the golf course, by a hedge at first, then on to a waymarker. Turn right here, make for a hedge corner, then continue in the same direction, with the hedge on your left, until you reach a stile and a track to Mickledale, the farm ahead.

Walk through the farmyard, past the farmhouse with its mullioned windows, and the ancient pump and sandstone byre. Behind you the ever-widening Mersey fans out into its estuary as you make for the road at Higher Mickledale Farm and turn left.

Immediately after passing the entrance to the first house turn right over a fence, its green paint flaking badly. Go down this field and turn right over a very rickety iron stepladder in the corner. Continue in the same direction down the next field, and then turn right again down a country lane. Where the road turns sharply left keep ahead down a track. Around you unfolds a landscape of gently undulating fields. Drop down to the road, turn right up the incline and then go right again down to Riley's Bank.

As you mount the stepladder ahead, an immaculately maintained farmhouse, once owned by a French abbot and dating from 1450, stands proudly, encircled by white fences and gates. Walk across the field, scrambling down to a further stepladder in this pretty, unspoilt valley. Keep on to

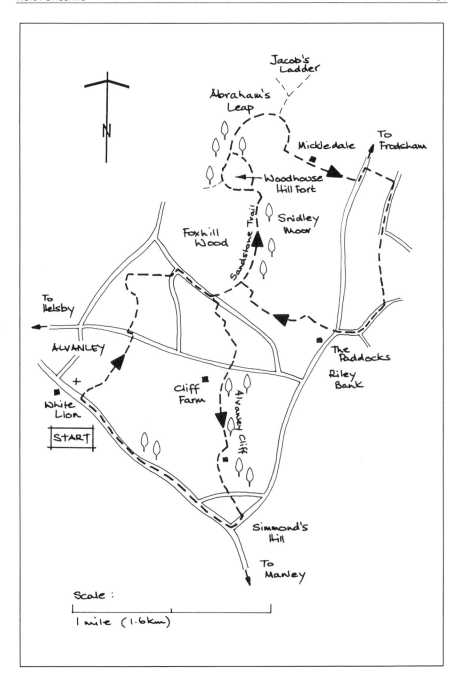

another stile and then follow the valley floor, hugging the bracken-strewn hillside until you turn right along a short, muddy cart-track.

At the end of this turn left down the side of the field, and go left again as you rejoin the Sandstone Trail. Turn left when you reach the Ridgeway, then right up steps into Ridgeway Wood, signposted to Delamere Forest. A rhapsody of birdsong greets you as you drop through this little wood and turn left alongside the stream. Leaves crunch crisply underfoot, and acrobatic grey squirrels sometimes perform high in the trees.

Cross the bridge out of the wood and follow the Sandstone Trail up the side of a field, turning left through the gap at the top. Motor cycle scramblers may be racing over the rough sandy ground nearby as you walk to wooden steps, cross a stile and continue round the next field.

Here, the 'magpie' walls of aptly-named Cliff Farm can be spotted sheltering under Alvanley Cliff as you cross the lane and stile opposite, walk over the grass to a further stile, then continue under the brow of the hill. Evidence of deserted sandstone quarries may also be seen while, on the lower ground, the sandy soil provides prolific potato crops. Turn right at the end of the field and then left, passing a brick and timber-framed hall, transported from the Nantwich area and rebuilt in this attractive setting. Cross another field to reach an unusual stile, the top arm acting as a lever.

Cross the road and the next stile to continue in the direction of Manley Common and Delamere Forest. The path is distinctly marked, even when crops are growing in the field, as it drops down to the lane where you turn right alongside the forbidding bulk of Simmond's Hill. Turn right again at the T-junction – the boundary of Alvanley and Manley – and wend your way towards revival in the White Lion's convivial atmosphere.

Winwick

Route: Winwick – Hermitage Green – Southworth Hall – Houghton Green – Peel Hall Park – Myddleton Lane

Distance: 7 miles

Start: Swan Tavern (SJ 605927)

By Car: Take the A49 north from Warrington. Cross over the M62 and, at the next roundabout, continue towards Newton-le-Willows. As you bear right into Golborne Road (in front of Winwick Church) the pub car park is on your right.

Swan Tavern – 01925 631416 (Chef & Brewer)

As signified by the date sign on the drainpipe, the Swan dates from 1898 when it was a coaching inn on the main road from Warrington to Wigan. The original pub stood higher up the road on the extension to the car park.

This pub is open from 11 am to 11pm each day. Bitters include Theakstons Best and John Smith's and there are also guest beers. Lagers include Foster's and Kronenberg. Draught Guinness is also served, and a choice of two ciders – Strongbow and Woodpecker.

All the food is freshly prepared on the premises and there is a choice of about twenty dishes on the 'specials' board each day. A substantial wine list is available.

Ramblers are always welcome in the bar, and the children's play area outside is well used during the summer months. There is also a function room which is often booked for small wedding parties, seminars or business conferences.

A lodge is now attatched to the Tavern and accommodation is available.

The Walk

This walk takes you in a wide circle through the countryside around Winwick. A village steeped in history, the tall spire of its ancient church is rarely out of sight.

Turn right as you leave The Swan down Newton Road, looking up as you pass the church tower to see the pig with a bell round its neck beside St Anthony. There are several explanations concerning its origin; one legend says that a pig was used to move the stones to this place when the chosen site for the church was altered. Another story is that this was the stonemason's cryptic way of putting the initials of St. Oswald's, Winwick (SOW)

The pig beside St Anthony on Winwick church

on the church. But perhaps the most plausible reason is simply that St. Anthony's mascot was a pig.

Cross the road at the traffic lights here and turn left towards Burtonwood, passing the entrance to Winwick Hospital – the church rectory until 1902 when it became an asylum. During both World Wars this was the largest military hospital in the country, but it is now closed. Turn right at the footpath sign; then walk down the grassy strip separating two fields. From here Vulcan's chimneys tower above flat fields, before you bear right, the hedge on your left. Cut into the little wood bordering the field along here, where a path brings you back onto Newton Road.

Turn left, and immediately right down Old Schoolhouse Lane, the tarmac giving way to a grassy path which turns sharp left away from bungalows. Keep ahead into the field, walking to the left of a hawthorn hedge and passing a pylon. As you continue up the grassy strip dividing two fields Parkgate Colliery appears prominently in front. Then pass the end of a hedge and keep ahead again down a grassy divide until, on reaching a facing hedge, you bear left to a cart-track which takes you down to the road.

Turn right here down Hermitage Green Lane, passing Hermitage Farm to reach The Hermit, an inn with an unusual sign and a splendid garden slide and tree house for children. Turn left at the pub and pass through the tiny hamlet of Hermitage Green, which encircles this particularly bad double bend. As you pass the last house, look over the fenced-in enclosure above the pond. This is St Oswald's Well. Reputed to be the spot where St. Oswald, saint and king of Northumbria, was slain, its water is deemed to have special healing powers.

Look out for the footpath sign on the right, where you climb stone steps to a

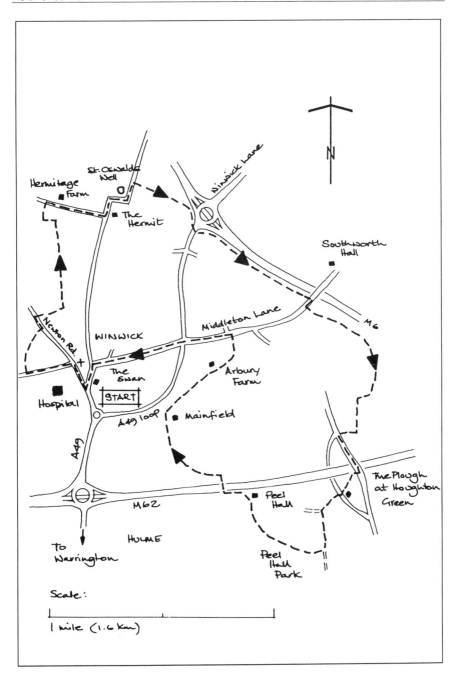

stile and then walk above a field. Keep in the same direction to cross two more stiles, before veering right down the fence when you reach the motorway slip road. You soon ascend a crisscross stile, and climb up steps in the embankment to the roundabout.

Continue in the same direction to cross the A49 loop, keeping the roundabout on your left. Then drop down steep steps and bear left over a stile. Continue down the edge of fields, with the motorway on your left, until you reach Middleton Lane.

On the far side of the motorway, where much quarrying has taken place, in 1980 an archaeological excavation exposed arrowheads and urns dating from about 1,500 BC. Here too stands the attractive, symmetrical building of Southworth Hall, its ancient, oaken door perhaps dating from the Civil War.

Turn right here. Then take the first opportunity to turn left, doubling back to pass a bungalow before going right along a footpath through the wood. After keeping ahead over a further stile, you can walk either side of the hawthorn hedge, then skirt the slip road until you leave the hedge at the footpath sign, veering over the field towards a motorway viaduct.

Skirt the pond on your right and climb up to the stile, clearly discernible beside an oak tree in the facing hedge. Go ahead along the strip of grass lying between two fields, then make a right-angled turn to the road. Here, you turn left to cross the motorway before descending steps on your right. At the bottom bear right, and then left down a path between rough fields and a hedgerow, which brings you to The Plough at Houghton Green – now a pub with a bowling green, but formerly a spinning mill.

Turn right and left here down Radley Lane, then bear left again after a short distance, and the track soon borders New Town property. At the entrance to Peel Hall Park bear right,then circle round derelict buildings before bearing right again to a pretty wood. Walk through this, then make for the back of Peel Hall Kennels, after which a grassy track takes you to the motorway footbridge.

Climb a stile and walk over the footbridge before bearing left along a wide, grassy path between crops. Skirt to the right of the wood ahead; then bear right again along a cart track to Mainfield, keeping ahead at the signpost on the way. After passing the farm with its noisy, chained dog, keep along the track to Arbury Farm, where both the spire of Warrington parish church (third highest in the country), and the gas works, can be easily spotted. Keep left at Arbury Croft down Arbury Road, and turn left again along Myddleton Lane.

After crossing over the motorway spur you walk back into Winwick, past the village school, itself a goodly age, but not so old as the first settlement in the area which dates back to Saxon times. Indeed, the cross-arm of a Celtic preaching cross, over 1,000 years old, is now preserved in the church. This cross would have stood on top of the hill long before any religious building was there.

Winwick Church

This ancient and splendidly-preserved church is well worth a visit. Dedicated to St. Oswald, King of Northumbria, it is mentioned in the Domesday Book of 1066 when the living belonged to Roger of Poitou, one of William the Conqueror's nobles. It later passed under the patronage of Nostel Priory before being owned by the Derby family, by which time it was a very wealthy living indeed.

Parts of the present building, which is made of local sandstone, date from 1330, and a 14th century font, perhaps damaged in the Civil War, can still be seen. Near it is a copy of the Vinegar Bible – so named because of a misprint in the heading to the twentieth chapter of St. Luke's Gospel, where the word 'vinegar' has been printed instead of 'vineyard'; thus making the title read 'The Parable of the Vinegar'!

Nearby too, in the richly-coloured east window of the north aisle, the story of King Oswald's life is depicted in stained glass and, in the main body of the church, the chancel was designed by the famous architect, Welby Pugin, who designed the Houses of Parliament. At the opposite side, in the Peter Legh chapel, there are brasses of both Peter Legh and his wife. After her untimely death he became a priest, and is depicted wearing a priest's vestments together with full armour, sword and spurs – a rare combination.

In the church there are booklets of the church's history both for adults and children. They tell its story in simple language and each cost but a few pence. You could peruse them at your leisure while relaxing at The Swan.

Mid Cheshire

Beeston Castle	Mostly on Farndon, Holt & Tattenhall SJ 45/55
Church Minshull	Winsford & Sandbach SJ 66/76
Foxtwist Green	Winsford & Sandbach SJ 66/76
Great Barrow	Chester (East) SJ 46/56
Raw Head	Farndon, Holt & Tattenhall SJ 45/55

There is no theme to this section; each walk differs greatly from its neighbour. An ancient castle, and outstanding views over the Cheshire Plain, complement more gentle stretches along either canal paths or a converted railway line, and places to visit in the area reflect this diversity.

Chester

No section on this part of the county would be complete without mention of Chester, Cheshire's ancient county town with its roots in Roman history. It would be difficult to do justice to the many places to visit within its walls: the Roman amphitheatre, a Cathedral founded by Benedictine monks, the impressive Norman interior of St. John's church, the Grosvenor Museum and Park, Eastgate with its ornately gilded clock tower and 'The Rows'. A 2-mile walk around the walls themselves, built in the 13th century to give extra protection from the Welsh, gives splendid views over the city and its race-course – the Roodee – and there's always a variety of boats to hire for a trip on the River Dee. Also, a few miles to the east of the city is Chester Zoo, where the combination of delightful gardens with a large collection of animals, birds and reptiles, provides an enjoyable day's outing.

Beeston Castle

Magnificent ruins crown a high craggy outcrop rising 300 feet above the plain below, and 500 feet above sea level. Built by Ranulf, Earl of Chester, in 1220 as a military stronghold to withstand Welsh attacks, its turbulent history includes plenty of fierce fighting during the Civil War, when it was eventually captured by the Roundheads.

You can climb up from the studded gate and bastion of its outer walls to cross the drawbridge spanning the moat, then look down the well, 370 feet deep, where Richard III is supposed to have buried treasure worth almost a million pounds. From the walls surrounding this courtyard eight counties are visible on a clear day. On the grassy slopes a labyrinth of hidden caves makes an ideal venue for hide and seek, and, in the car park, a snack bar operates during the summer months.

Beeston Castle is signposted off the A49 south of Tarporley and is open most days. Telephone Bunbury (01829) 260464 for details.

The Candle Factory (Cheshire Workshops)

Here you can see craftsmen at work fashioning exotic and decorative candles and, in the summer, children are able to make a candle of their own to take home.

Take the A534 from Chester and the Cheshire Workshops are signed at the Burwardsley turn to the left. They are open daily from 10am. Telephone: Tattenhall (01829) 70401.

Bunbury Mill

This 17th century water mill has been restored to full working order, and flour made on the premises can be purchased.

Take the road down to the canal from Bunbury and the mill is on the left. It is open at certain times during the summer months. Telephone: Penketh (01925) 724321.

The Sandstone Trail

The Sandstone Trail is a 32-mile, long-distance footpath which snakes its way along the central Cheshire ridge. Intermittently bisecting the plain, it stretches from Beacon Hill, above Frodsham, to Grindley Brook, near Whitchurch. To make the route easy to follow distinctive yellow trail markers show a footprint engraved with the letter 'S'. A number of the pubs in this book pass along, or near, the Sandstone Trail, and several of the walks include sections of its route, which passes through a variety of scenery, craggy hillsides giving way to shadowy forests or lush meadowland.

Travelling southwards, the Trail starts at Beacon Hill, where an Armada beacon once stood to warn of invasion. It then drops down the steeply eroded curves of Jacob's Ladder and follows the Overton ridge, which yields extensive views over the industrial Mersey estuary. The White Lion at Alvanley could be a useful stopping place at the end of this section.

The Trail continues through Delamere Forest, a series of bucks and bows then taking the walker over Primrose Hill, after which the woodland is left behind for the windswept fields around Willington. Dairy cattle predominate as you by-pass Tarporley and reach the Shropshire Union Canal (Chester branch), where the nearby Shady Oak offers sustenance.

After skirting the precipitous outcrop topped by Beeston Castle, a walk through the wooded uplands of Peckforton Estate will bring you within a stone's throw of The Pheasant at Higher Burwardsley. Here, accommodation is on offer at roughly the half-way point of the Trail.

After this you soon climb to Rawhead, the highest point (746 feet above sea level), where spectacular views over the plain below extend as far as the Welsh foothills, and the eroded sandstone cliffs and caves are particularly red and dramatic because of the rock's strong iron content. After traversing the hillsides around Bickerton and Maiden Castle the route drops down to fertile, friesian-grazed pastures. The tiny church of Old Chad offers a breezy view before a gentle walk takes you down to Willeymoor Lock Tavern and the Shropshire Union Canal (Llangollen Branch). From here the towpath is followed to its end at the Shropshire border, where the Horse and Jockey offers both food and drink.

The Whitegate Way

Signposted from the A556 near Sandiway, the Whitegate Way is a sandy bridleway, six miles in length, which follows the obsolete railway line between Winsford and Cuddington. Axed in the Beeching Cuts, this line was built in the 1880s to transport salt from the Winsford mines to the junction with the Chester/Manchester railway line at Cuddington.

Provisions such as coal, bricks and straw, for use in the local community, were also offloaded at Whitegate Station, which has now been converted into a car park and picnic area. In the railway era's heyday, twelve trains stopped there each day, and passengers too travelled on the line – a single ticket in 1930 costing less than 4d. At the station a height gauge can still be seen – once used to check whether heavily-laden trucks would clear the bridges.

The surrounding countryside comprises flower-stippled meadows, shady copses and sandy heaths, while fir-fringed pools offer a haven to many varieties of birdlife. Along the Way itself, the sloping banks of cuttings are covered in harebell, hawkweed and toadflax, while butterflies, moths and dragonflies are enticed to breed in the more sheltered places.

Walking along Whitegate Way is always easy, with no steep gradients. Wheelchairs and prams are catered for, and a three-mile section is also open for horse riders – an ideal ride for the novice.

Beeston Castle

Route: Bate's Mill Bridge — Crimes Lane — Moathouse Farm — Peckforton Estate — Beeston village — Beeston Market — Shropshire Union Canal

Distance: 8 miles

Start: Shady Oak (SJ 533603)

By Car: Take the A54 (the Northwich road) from Chester, and branch right onto the A51 from the Tarvin by-pass. At Clotton turn right onto Crooked Lane and, after passing through the hamlet of Huxley, take the next right turn to the Shady Oak.

Shady Oak – 01829 733159 (Pub Estates)

The Shady Oak, which is about 150 years old, has had many landlords in its history. Ducks have always thrived on the canal here, and two swans come to produce their cygnets each year. Horses and a donkey in the adjacent field are also a big attraction for children, and the tiny orchard has swings, a slide and a tree for climbing.

Ramblers tend to go into the tap room where the floor is uncarpeted. It is the oldest part of the pub. Here, an elderly lady died in her chair, and a ghost is said to wander round at night. Dave Thomason, who worked here for over twelve years and lived locally all his life, remembers a toffee cabinet in this bar which dispensed both chocolate, and such unlikely delicacies as cockles, mussels and pickled eggs. The pub was eventually extended to provide a spacious lounge bar; the sunny conservatory overlooking garden and canal has been a recent addition.

Food is served every day with roasts on Sundays. There is also a selection of children's meals, and 'specials' are advertised on the blackboard.

John Smiths is the main beer served at this Pub Estates pub. Draught Guinness is also available and four draught lagers.

The Walk

Leave the pub and turn left over Bate's Mill bridge. The old mill was a trout farm for a time, and now has its own electricity generator worked by the water-wheel visible below the road. Continue down the road towards Beeston Castle, crossing the railway, passing cottages, then looking out for a footpath on the right signposted to Crimes Lane. Walk over the field here, veering slightly right towards an oak tree in the facing hedge, where a plank stile spans a deep ditch. Keep ahead over the next field to stiles either side

Enjoying a drink in the sunshine outside the Shady Oak

of a grassy track. Continue on, making for evergreen trees and another stile. Walk beside these trees to pass a pond, then climb over a further stile to reach Lower Rock Farm, where you keep ahead to the road.

Here, follow the footpath sign to Horsley Lane and Wickson Lane. Beeston and Peckforton castles loom ahead, so different in style and origin, as you follow the perfectly-shaped hawthorn hedge to the stile at the field's end. Magnificent crops of sweetcorn and healthy friesian herds dominate the Beeston area, with an occasional crop of rape to add colour and variety. Continue down the next field to a stile and plank bridge, then turn left at the oak here along a track of grass and gravel (signposted to Horsley Lane).

Leave this track shortly to cross to a stile in a barbed wire fence. Then pass between two oaks and keep ahead parallel with the hedge to a stile at the far end of the field. Cross the next field to a stile between oaks in the facing hedge. After this you go ahead down a dirt track with a good view of the Elizabethan farmhouse at Moathouse Farm, dwarfed by its massive brick chimney. A mineral spring, noted for the purity of its water, surfaces in the private grounds here. You soon pass renovated outbuildings and an old byre of rough-hewn sandstone before turning right along the road.

After a short distance go left through the gate into Peckforton Estate woods, following the Sandstone Trail towards Bulkeley Hill. Forestry and pheasant rearing still take place on the estate, and many of the birds can be seen running on their spindly legs both in the woods and on the adjacent fields. At the first junction continue towards Bulkeley Hill, perhaps assailed by the aromatic smell of newly sawn timber from the clearing here. You soon glimpse the cottage roofs in Higher Burwardsley and the craggy, sandstone cliffs of Raw Head. Where the track drops down to the right you turn left up a little path to follow the Sandstone Trail towards Bulkeley Hill. As the path climbs diagonally up the side of the hill crown galls grow like warts on the gnarled trunks of ancient oaks.

Climb over the stile at the summit and your way is ahead, leaving the Sandstone Trail which turns right. This right-of-way, which cuts off a corner, at first passes through a plantation of Christmas trees before it enters a wilder area of gorse, bracken and bramble over another stile. A marshy area of bog grass, reeds and moss brings you to a main track by a small pond, where you turn left. Passing under the supposedly haunted bridge down here can be an eerie experience. Ignore the notice saying 'Strictly Private' at the second turning on the left and walk to the signpost. You are not going to trespass but, from this vantage point, the hidden pathway which cuts over stiles and fields down to the road can be seen.

To your right is Peckforton, a village of pretty Tudor cottages, its fox hunt the oldest in England. But you turn left, and have a glimpse of Peckforton Mere nestling amongst grassy slopes as you pass the sandstone walls and cobbled drive of Garden Cottage. Just before the lodge gates and ancient oak (the perimeter of its trunk measuring 21 feet) you turn right over a stile towards Beeston Moss and Bunbury. Veer left across this field with Beeston and Peckforton castles to your left. Although Peckforton Castle is really a sham, built as the country seat of Lord Tollemache in the mid-19th century from locally quarried sandstone, it is a perfect replica of a Norman castle and is dominated by a keep sixty feet high.

The four trees ahead are remnants of a hedge that once divided this field. Pass through the middle of them and, as you breast the crown of the hill, a stile will come into view beside a gate. The ponds here provide a home for geese which may honk balefully as they rise from the placid surface. Walk along a broad, grassy ride into the wood; then leave it over a stile, and bear right to a cart-track, where you turn left. At the farm bear right to the road, then go left for a short way to a stile signposted to Bunbury.

As you walk over this field to a second stile, the castle walls, battlements and gatehouse of Beeston Castle are clearly visible in three tiers up the hillside. The right-of-way is straight across the next field and, with luck, there will be a narrow path between the crops. If not, make for the lone telegraph

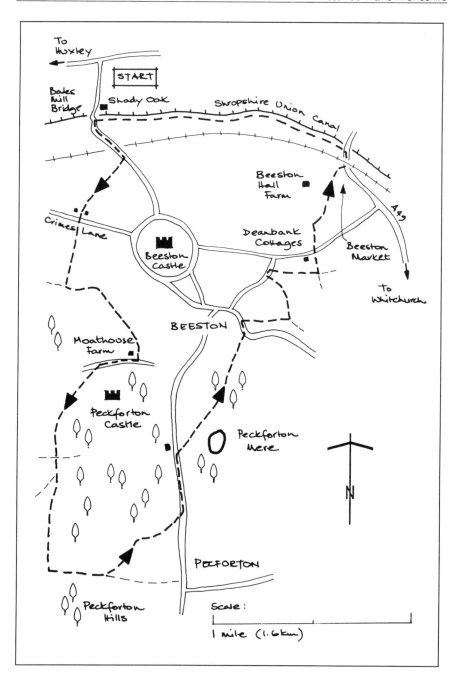

To Huxley

START

Bates Mill Bridge

Shady Oak

Shropshire Union Canal

Beeston Hall Farm

Deanbank Cottages

Crimes Lane

Beeston Castle

Beeston Market

To Whitchurch

A49

BEESTON

Moathouse Farm

Peckforton Castle

Peckforton Mere

PECKFORTON

Peckforton Hills

N

Scale:

1 mile (1.6km)

pole and the stile to its right in the facing hedge. Do not climb over this but turn left alongside the hedge. Then, at a dog-leg bend, strike out over the field, aiming for the house where a plank bridge and signpost lie to the right of an ivy-shrouded oak.

Turn right along the road, and immediately right again towards Bunbury and the A49. Walk down the side of this long field to a stile, which takes you onto a grassy track where you turn left to Deanbank Cottages. Cross the country lane and the cattle grid here, then continue down the farm road towards Beeston Hall Farm. You soon turn right over a stile and drop down through a plantation of evergreens to skirt a field. After crossing a final meadow climb over a stile into Beeston cattle market (the Smithfield of the north), which is held every Wednesday and is well worth visiting.

Turn left along the A49, passing under the railway bridge and over the Gowy before dropping down to the towpath on your left. This is the Chester Branch of the Shropshire Union Canal, built in 1775 to link the manufacturing towns of the Midlands with the Mersey ports. Wharton's lock and bridge exudes a rustic charm, and the foundations of the lock-keeper's cottage – destroyed by a bomb in the Second World War – can still be seen, together with the remains of an old mill on the Gowy's banks. A gentle stroll from here completes the walk, taking you back to the Shady Oak for welcome refreshment.

Church Minshull

Route: Church Minshull – Shropshire Union Canal – Hunter's Bridge – Lea Green – B5074

Distance: 6 miles

Start: The Badger (SJ666605)

By Car: Take the B5074 south from Winsford. The pub is on the right in the village of Church Minshull, after a sharp, right-hand bend. Ample parking is to be found by the post office and general store attached to the pub.

The Badger – 01270 522607 (Paramount)

Situated in the centre of the tiny hamlet of Church Minshull, the Badger is a Grade 2 listed building of historic and architectural interest. Built in 1760 as a thatched-roofed farmhouse overlooking a cobbled street, water was supplied by a garden well and a stream running through the cellar, from which a tunnel is reputed to connect with the church.

Later on, The Badger became a coaching inn, a stopping point for the weekly coach service operating between the salt towns of Nantwich and Northwich. Even when this terminated, the tradition was upheld until the 1950s by a coach travelling between the two towns on one day each year.

Although this is badger country and, in the grounds behind the beer garden there are at least two setts, the original name of the pub was the Brook Arms. The story goes that an artist, commissioned to redesign the squire's coat-of-arms, incorporated a badger into it. This delighted the man so much that he not only kept it but altered the name of the pub too.

The Badger was once notable as a bikers' pub, when its jukebox was rumoured to be the largest in the country. Then the local petrol station stood where the restaurant now is, the place where the hand pump used to be still evident in the wall. The adjoining shop is now also owned by the licensee, which enables boat people enjoying an evening drink or a bar meal at the pub, to stock up with groceries ready for an early start next morning.

Ramblers, who are always welcome, together with dogs and children, tend to use the Snu which has 12-inch floorboards, pine pews and a bar made of York stone. Pictures of wild life adorn the walls and the pub also tends to act as a focal point for country pursuits, regularly hosting meetings of the local Beagles, and the Cheshire Hunt visiting twice a year.

Although the restaurant is well known throughout Cheshire and the surrounding counties, there are many appetising dishes on the bar menu as

Salvation and damnation in Church Minshull

well. These often vary with the season, game being particularly popular in the winter months.

A Real Ale pub, The Badger has a large array of pumps lined up all round the bar. All the beer is cask and includes Boddingtons, IPA Flowers bitter and a selection of lagers.

The Walk

Walk down the road opposite the car park past the house named Church Fields. You soon cross the meandering River Weaver and turn left, crossing a field from which you exit over a stile in the opposite corner. If this is made difficult because of barbed wire, continue to the farmhouse of Old Hoolgrave Farm and turn left over the well-maintained cobbles.

On reaching the Shropshire Union Canal (Middlewich Branch) at Bridge 11 turn left along the canal bank, where there is a delightful view of St. Bartholomew's church, dating from 1702. The village nestles snugly around it while, in the foreground, the River Weaver winds among lush, green pastures grazed by herds of plump, friesian cows.

Eardswick Hall is over to your right as you stroll easily along the grassy bank. Farm buildings dot the countryside, surrounded on all sides by undulating meadows. After Bridge 16 the canal narrows where once was a bridge, and then you pass brick stables and a deserted house, its wooden shutters still showing a pretty flower design. Just past here you come to Bridge 19 where you leave the canal through a small, black gate, and a track goes off to the Verdin Arms, which offers both food and drink. To continue the walk, however, turn right into a field, passing two sturdy oaks on your left before dropping down to a stile.

Cross the next field and exit over the fence in the opposite hedge. Then walk diagonally up the following field to turn right alongside the wood. Negotiate a fence into a further field, and a stile into a final one – from where the footbridge over the Weaver comes into view. Known as Hunters' Bridge, it takes you high above the river, and you then walk up the field beside a barbed wire fence. Climb over the gate at the end and continue up a grassy track, soon turning right onto a cart track, which becomes a road and passes Lea Green Villa Farm.

You can, if you so wish, continue along this road, then turn left along the busy B5074 back to The Badger. However, the route through Sandicroft Wood is detailed below as a steep but pretty alternative, which cuts out much of the road walking.

Turn left down the drive to Lea Green Hall. Continue through the farmyard, then turn right down the side of a huge field to a stile into Sandicroft Wood. A pretty path drops steeply down through this and continues alongside the River Weaver. Leave the wood at a well-built stile, then cross two more to reach the busy B5074. Turn left and continue with care back to Church Minshull and The Badger.

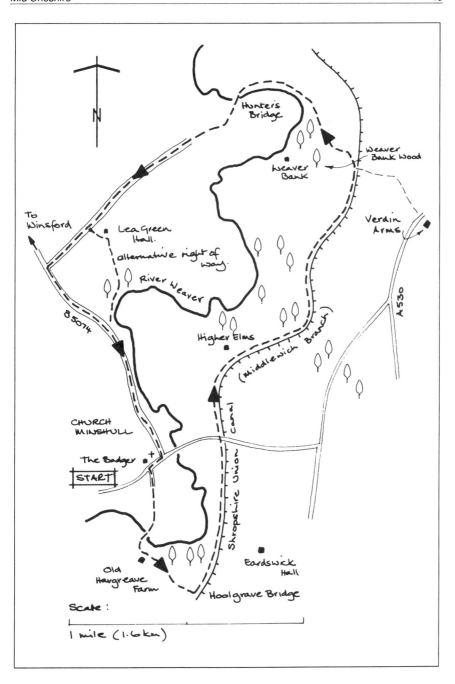

Hunter's Bridge

Weaver Bank Wood

Weaver Bank

Verdin Arms

To Winsford

Lea Green Hall.

alternative right of way.

River Weaver

B 5074

A 530

Higher Elms

(Middlewich Branch)

CHURCH MINSHULL

The Badger

START

Shropshire Union Canal

Eardswick Hall

Old Hargreave Farm

Hoolgrave Bridge

Scale :

1 mile (1.6 km)

Foxtwist Green

Route: Beauty Bank – Whitegate – Sherratt's Rough – Newchurch Common – Whitegate Way – Martonsands

Distance: 5 miles

Start: The Plough (SJ 624682)

By Car: Take the A54 from Winsford towards Kelsall. At Salterswall bear right towards Sandiway. Then take the right fork at Martonsands and The Plough is the next right turn.

The Plough – 01606 889455 (Robinson's)

Amidst field-flanked lanes north-west of Winsford, and not far from The Beeches (perhaps the centre of Cheshire), stands the faded signpost to The Plough. Down a No Through Road atop Beauty Bank, this unspoilt pub, with its jovial regulars and helpful publican, hides in the tiny hamlet of Foxtwist Green. Ramblers are always welcome, usually taking their muddy boots into the back bar where the floor is still flagged.

As with many country pubs, The Plough was once a farm, but is shown on a map dating from 1910 as a pub. Once part of the extensive Delamere estate, both pub and cottages in the area are exempt from water rates. This dates from when the authorities first wanted to pipe water through the area and, as a condition of permission being granted, Lord Delamere stipulated that the people who lived on the estate should never be rated.

The only fight anyone remembers here was when two dogs took a dislike to each other and had to be separated. And many other stories of the area are told by Les Brockley, a local builder, and his cronies. They remember when the bungalow opposite used to be a pop factory called Whitegate Minerals; when, at the junction with the road to Whitegate a tailor used to work from a little wooden hut; and how, at one time the Irish used to come over to work on the local farms. Harvesting or digging potatoes during the day, at night they would sleep in barns, eating bread and cheese for their supper.

Other stories tell of the Second World War when the Prince of Wales, and other members of the royal family, often visited the pub when staying at nearby Cassia Lodge, as also did Eisenhower. The Americans had a large army camp nearby at Pettypool, and one young American soldier landed in Liverpool, checked into camp, and then ended up at The Plough for the evening. Unused to the strength of British beer, he staggered out of the pub and ended up in the barbed wire fence opposite, eventually having to be cut free. The beer is still strong, and served traditionally from the wood. Robin-

Licensee and regulars outside The Plough at Foxtwist Green

son's Best Mild and Best Bitter are always available, plus an array of other Robinson's beers such as Old Stockport which are interchanged.

The Plough used to have only a six-day licence because, in about 1870, Lady Delamere was incensed by the noise of drunken revelry when she was leaving Whitegate Church one Sunday morning. To put a stop to any further merry-making on the Sabbath she ruled that no alcohol should be sold in the area on that day, and it was a long time before this was rescinded.

Lunches are served every day and the menu is varied, including dishes that are all home-made.

The Walk

Continue up the lane, then turn left between houses down a rough road to a stile ahead and a signpost to Foxtwist Green. Walk down the left side of the field to another stile, over which you descend into the next field. Keep ahead again to cross a further stile and drop down into a valley. Then cross a bridge over a deep ditch before walking up a field and, near its end, turning right over a stile in the hedge. Stay in the same direction as before, walking alongside a holly hedge and turning right when you reach the road.

At Swallows' Nest, climb over the stile to the right of the drive, then walk alongside the hedge, passing the house. Negotiate a stile and keep beside a holly hedge to the next stile. Keep ahead along the side of the next field,

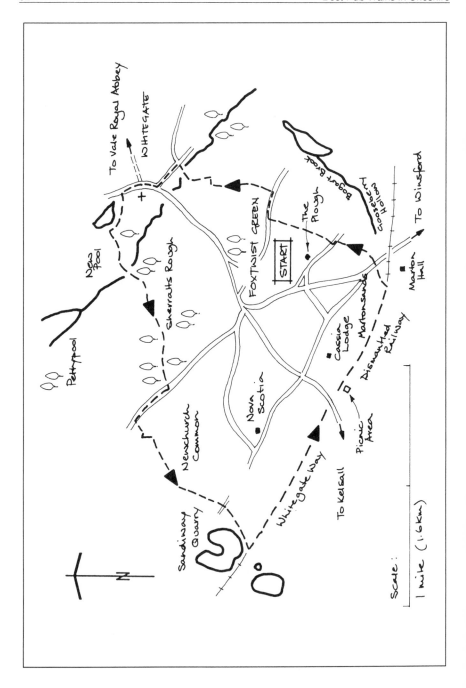

The lodge at the main entrance to Vale Royal Abbey

then turn right at the far end and go through a gap in the hedge. Keep ahead across the next field, drop down to a narrow gap by a gate and bear right over a stream. From here turn right and left to climb between beech hedges, then ascend steep steps onto Grange Lane.

Turn left into Whitegate village, where Whitegate House was once a pub called the Rifleman Inn. It lost its licence in 1870 when Lady Daresbury again objected to the drunken behaviour of its customers as she was leaving church one Sunday morning. And it was after this episode that all the other pubs in the area were only granted a six-day licence for many years. Turn right onto Whitegate Lane towards St Mary's church. Avoid the blind corner here by walking quietly up through the churchyard, passing the church and then continuing down a grassy path between an avenue of yews to a gate into the car park at the far end.

To the right of the church is the main entrance to Vale Royal Abbey, the white gate giving the village its name. In the grounds of Vale Royal once stood a glorious Cistercian Abbey – the largest in England – built of sandstone from the quarry at Eddisbury and timber from Delamere Forest. It was instigated by Prince Edward (son of Henry III), a thanksgiving for his safe return from the Crusades after his ship had been struck by a severe gale. He laid the foundation stone himself in 1277 after he became King Edward I. Unfortunately, it was totally razed to the ground by Henry VIII during his dissolution of the monasteries.

Later, the Delamere family built a mansion on the site; its hall, seventy feet long, had carved oak roof beams, and pictures by Rubens graced the walls. The park itself covered 800 acres, and had magnificent avenues of giant trees and lakes with rare water fowl. Two eagles were kept and legend said that when the eagles disappeared then the family would soon follow. This did, in fact, occur for the eagles died soon after one another, and at present the house is a ruin.

Leave the car park by a stile in the far corner, after which a path continues down to New Pool – a pleasant retreat for anglers. Grey squirrels scamper here and there as you bear left to skirt this pretty spot. Keep alongside the pool to cross the old original stream, where water runs off from the lake into the wood, then turn left alongside the next beck instead of crossing the wooden footbridge. This artificial stream was dug out of the sandy soil in about 1984, draining water from Pettypool to maintain a high level for the anglers here.

Over to your right is a hill of very sandy soil, ideal for use as a building material. The locals are hoping that permission won't be granted for quarrying here. The redness of the soil is very evident in the stream's banks as you walk along beside it, keeping your eyes open for a yellow arrow on the grotesque remains of a tree, where you need to turn left onto a permissive path. (If you reach a stile and bridge you've missed it!)

You soon cross one of two wooden bridges standing side by side, then continue along a well-maintained path, stone chippings having been used very successfully to combat the mud. An uncanny silence pervades this woodland as you climb between Scots pine and bracken, veering right then left. The occasional twitter of birdsong is almost an intrusion. Pine needles cushion your footfalls as you descend to a clearing and turn right along a wide, stony track. (It is now possible to bear right a little earlier to cut off this corner.) You soon pass warnings of overhead electricity cables and then continue through the wood known as Sherratts Rough.

When you reach the road turn right and, after a quarter-of-a-mile, turn left down the rough road to Birchdale and Lapwing Hall Farm. You soon leave this road, turning right down a footpath which runs between a paddock and holly hedge. You are now walking towards Newchurch Common which, in the Middle Ages, was common land used for the grazing of cattle and pigs.

Climb over a stile into a field and then keep ahead until you turn left along the far side of the field to a farm track. Cross this and the stile ahead to walk through a slim coppice of pine and silver birch. A hedge of gorse shelters your left side and to your right is a bank, from the top of which there is a superb view of a huge, water-filled quarry and its abundant bird life.

Cross a rough road and bear left over a stile, then cross a rough road and the stile opposite. Follow the path straight down the field ahead (ignoring one veering right) until you reach a bridleway. Keep forward along it, then bear left to the Whitegate Way at a clearing. Turn left along this. The separate walkers' path is sheltered here by an embankment, the horse riders enjoying the view from the top. Almost a mile further on, you walk under a road bridge, to which wooden beams offer extra support. Keep ahead towards Martonsands, passing Whitegate Station, where there are toilets and a picnic area.

To the right lies Martin Grange, a farm since the 13th century, and Cassia Lodge lies far to your left. Built during Queen Anne's reign, it was once the home of the Earl of Enniskillen, and King Edward VII, when the Prince of Wales, often visited there. Take the second turn left to Martonsands – the one immediately after the right turn to Marton Hole and Chester Lane. To your right here is moated Marton Hall.

From here drop down wide, rough-hewn steps onto a path which leads to a road. Cross this and follow the footpath to Beauty Bank, climbing over the stile there and wending your way up the sandy hill. Below, Bogart Brook runs through Gooseberry Hollow and there used to be a saying in these parts, 'Foxes grow fat on rabbits' – the 'foxes' referring to poachers who made a good, if illegal, living around here. Some think that the name Foxtwist was derived from this saying. Climb over a stile at the hill's summit and turn right down a farm lane. Turn left at Hares Clough and you will soon be back at The Plough.

Great Barrow

Route: Little Barrow – Irons Lane – Park Hall – Mill Lane – Great Barrow – Ferma Lane – Barrow Hill

Distance: 5 miles

Start: The Foxcote (SJ 470699)

By Car: Take the A56 east from Chester, and turn right along the B5132 towards Great Barrow. The Foxcote is on the left in about 1.5 miles.

The Foxcote – 01244 301343 (In Partnership)

High up on breezy Broomhill as the road starts to run down through Little Barrow, stands The Foxcote. Originally a cottage farmhouse, its sturdy sandstone foundations are set deep into the hillside. During its 250 years as a pub it has had three names. At first known as The Snig after the horse which carried coal from the railway nearby, in the cellar below, where the horse was stabled, the original rings are still attached to the wall. The pub then became The Railway – the name by which it is still known locally.

However, in the 1980s it seems to have been Greenall Whitley policy to give many of their pubs upmarket names, and so The Railway became The Foxcote. One redeemable feature, however, is that it has retained its railway connections, for the Great Western Railway had a number of engines named after manors, one of which, Foxcote Manor, gave the pub its new name.

Northgate Station in Chester was one of the termini when the railway running nearby was built by the Cheshire Lines Committee. This was also the last line in the country to be nationalised.

Trains still thunder past on the line a short distance down the hill and, perhaps in deference to its origin, the station, although now converted to a private house, boasts a train-topped weather vane.

Until recent years the pub only consisted of one small bar and two front rooms, but a spacious extension now provides a second bar and pleasant lounge, with sweeping views over Broomhill and across the plain to the sphinx-like features of Helsby Hill, taking in three counties altogether.

All the food is fresh and home-made, with meals served seven days a week, lunchtime and evening. The extensive menu includes traditional favourites, home-made sausages and fresh fish. Pickles and chutneys are all home-made and vegetarian choices are made to order, usually at the whim of the guest. Children have their own menu and there are at least ten des-

Rough-hewn stone steps drop down off Barrow Hill. *(Photo: Cheshire Life)*

serts on offer every day, with temptations such as apple and toffee meringue and home-made ice cream. There is a play area outside for children when the weather is fine.

A function room can cater for forty if there is a private party, and ramblers are always welcome. Beers vary and guest beers are a great feature.

The Walk

As you turn right down Broomhill Lane notice the bricked up window high in the cottage wall – relic of 'window tax' days. After passing Broomhill Cottage, turn right at the road junction and continue up a lane, where the tall, dry-stone wall, festooned with ivy, is topped by a hawthorn hedge.

Bear left into Irons Lane, and then left again up some steps and over a stile, after which you walk down the field and negotiate another stile before turning right into a farm lane. Here, keep ahead past byres, barns and a dilapidated farmhouse to a stile into a field. Then walk along the hedge to another stile, and cross the field ahead in the slight dip which leads to a stile in the facing hedge. Continue over the next field to a further stile, then keep along the side of the field beyond that, noting the oaks, dotted at intervals along the hawthorn hedge, which offer both shade for cattle and nesting places for birds.

An ash tree guards the next stile, then you pass an alder as you continue alongside the hedge to the oak at the next stile. A further stile stands next to a steel gate, and you then bear left to a stile and rudimentary bridge over a stream, after which you continue along a grassy path, then past cottages to turn left at Irons Lane.

You soon turn right over a stile just past an oak tree, and walk up the field to a stile by another oak. Keep ahead again to a further stile supported by rough hewn stone pillars, then cross the field diagonally to a gate in the corner (to the right of an oak) and from there to a triangle of roads, where you turn left.

Walk to the bend and turn right down a No Through Road, crossing a hugely meandering stream, then turn right over a stile before reaching Park Hall. Many of the farms in Cheshire are called halls – which often makes them sound grander than they actually are! Cross through the hedge as you pass the farmhouse, then go over a stile into the next field. Keep in the same direction to another stile, and walk ahead again until you turn right halfway down the hedge over a plank bridge and stile.

Smoke curls up from the cottage chimneys of Great Barrow as you keep down the hedge on your right towards the village. The noise of rushing wa-

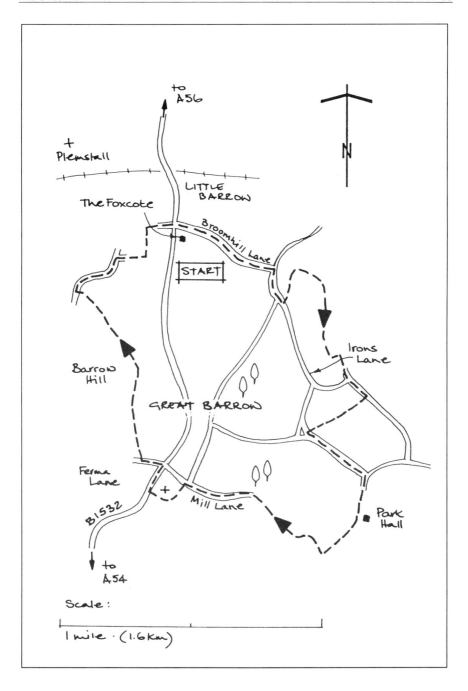

ter greets you as you drop over the stile out of this field and descend steps to a mud-based track. Here, turn left past the derelict, ivy-clad mill – sadly burnt down one drizzly Tuesday in August 1970.

Carry on down Mill Lane, lined with a miscellany of cottages, to the old village pump and lamp. The pump was in use until 1936 when piped water was laid on, and it was restored in 1977 to mark the queen's Silver Jubilee. Turn left away from it down a footpath past Hall Lane Cottage. Jasmine and berberis trail delicately over the sandstone wall before you pass through a kissing gate and walk on a grassy track beside the churchyard wall.

Many of the village streets converge around this area, some cutting through sheer rock faces. The church, dedicated to Saint Bartholomew, is perpendicular in style, with a fine old sundial in the churchyard. A hammerbeam roof tops the Jacobean nave, which has a 'bull's eye' window and houses an octagonal font made of fiery red sandstone. In the tower stands a Georgian chest and, as you pass by, the church clock may tonk out the time. Bear right up a lane past Blue Pig Cottage, then turn right past chapel and chapel house until a left turn at the village school takes you into Ferma Lane.

Take the first right turn along here to walk along the summit of Barrow Hill. Ahead is an industrial view of the Stanlow oil refineries and the industrial landscape of Ellesmere Port; on one side, the flat plain leads away to the distant Welsh Hills and, the backbone of hills on the other, supports the Sandstone Trail. The Peckforton Hills also make an exclamation mark with the Beeston Castle outcrop and, further north, the TV aerial stands high on Primrose Hill, pointing the way to the Overton Hills, which end abruptly with their sheer descent into Frodsham.

At a house turn left over a stile, dropping down to the plain over a second stile, then on down the side of a field to another stile in a hedge. You then turn right along a grassy track which bends right, then left, and can be very muddy.

Look out for a sight of Plemstall Church along here, peeping out of the trees. Inside is the most exquisite wood carving, all crafted by a former Vicar. Cut off a corner by turning right at a footpath sign, and climbing up the side of a field to bear left at an obsolete gatepost. Continue beside the hedge until you drop down steps to a farm road and turn right up to The Foxcote.

Rawhead

Route: Higher Burwardsley — Sandstone Trail — Rawhead — Bulkeley Hill — Rock Cottage

Distance: 5.5 miles

Start: There is only a small car park at the Pheasant Inn but a stone's throw up the road is the Candle Factory, which is well worth a visit and has huge parking facilities. (In summer, children can even make their own candles.) (SJ 523565)

By Car: Take the A534 west from Nantwich. After passing Foxes Bistro and dropping down Gallantry Bank, turn right towards Harthill and Burwardsley. You soon pass through Harthill, then take the next right turn to Burwardsley. At the outskirts of the village turn right and stay on this road — passing the church. Then keep right until you see The Pheasant ahead, where you turn right again to park at the Candle Factory.

The Pheasant Inn – 01829 770434 (Free House)

Although once a farm The Pheasant Inn has been a pub since the 17th century when, as part of the Carden Estate, it was called the Carden Arms. Nestling amongst the Peckforton Hills, its half-timbered, sandstone buildings have been beautifully maintained. The oldest part of the pub is the bar area, its array of gleaming bottles reflecting off the old oak beams, and the biggest log fire in Cheshire bisects the lounge bar.

The small car park was once a midden and, in the sheltered courtyard, bear and badger baiting used to take place. There was dancing too, in the barn on a Saturday night, to music provided by the village band – a drummer, a concertina-player and a fiddler. At one time elms stood protectively at the pub's front door, but these, alas, were killed by Dutch Elm disease. Sadly the parrot, an Amazon blue which used to imitate chickens from its cage in the bay window, has died. So you will no longer be greeted by its cheery, 'Hello'.

The pub is justly proud of its reputation for food. All the dishes are home-made using fresh ingredients. Nothing is frozen. There are three Real Ales which are changed regularly. The many wines on offer can be bought by the glass or the bottle. The bar is open all day, every day. Food is served all day at the weekend, and from noon to 2.30 pm and in the evening during the week.

Walkers are very welcome at anytime, and groups with prior notice. The

Once a farm, The Pheasant Inn nestles among the Peckforton Hills

small room behind the main bar was the original farmhouse kitchen. With its old oak beams, sandstone walls and traditional cooking range, it offers charm, comfort and character for that special occasion. The conservatory is pleasant too — a bright room where you can shelter from the wind while enjoying the sun.

The Pheasant Inn's Real Ale includes draught Bass, Timothy Taylor and Old Dog, although the beers are constantly being changed. It also has a large variety of fine wines in its well-stocked bar. The conservatory is open all day every day for families and walkers, and will serve a variety of food as well as afternoon teas during the summer.

Conveniently situated halfway along the Sandstone Trail, in addition to its other facilities The Pheasant Inn provides attractive bed and breakfast accommodation, both for those walking the Trail and others wishing to spend a holiday in the area. Some rooms are in the converted barn and have glorious views over the Cheshire Plain to Wales, a bathroom en suite where you can ease away those aches and pains, and a colour TV. The barn, with its steeply pitched roof and stone coping above the gable ends, is a typical Tudor building and a mounting block can still be seen outside.

The Walk

Drop down the hill from The Pheasant Inn, passing the tiny Methodist chapel dating from 1843 and then the estate cottages of Meshach and Shadrach, so named, apparently, when the owners of the Bolesworth estate went through a religious phase – but what happened to Abendigo? Once Shadrach's name was, more aptly perhaps, Lilac Cottage, and a row of lilacs bordered the quiet country lane.

About halfway along the wood down here turn left over a stile and climb the steps up through the trees until you bear right below the summit. Walk along beneath protruding overhangs of stratified sandstone, where you get a good view of the old village school, now a much used outdoor education centre for Cheshire schools. Next door is the village church with its diminutive spire, and rustic cottages cluster below as you round the end of the hill and climb up steps to a stile.

Burwardsley is actually mentioned in the Domesday Book as having a population of nine, and many of its fields have Norman names dating from that time. It is thought that people settled here because it was a natural clearing in the forest, and there was plenty of water from wells, springs and brooks. During the 19th century many of its cottagers were involved in glove making at home, and there were no fewer than five shoemakers.

Keep along the hedge and take the left fork to another stile, after which you drop down the field, passing two placid donkeys, to a wooden bridge and a stile onto the road. Turn right here and walk down to the bottom of the hill, where you cross the stile on your left – the route signposted to the Sandstone Trail and Rawhead.

Keep alongside the dip and marshy stream (crossing a vague track down from a gate) until you reach a wood and go over a stile into it. Climb up through this to exit by a further stile, and then cross the field ahead in the direction of the arrow. With luck an indentation in the grass may provide you with a line to follow until you see a stile over the electric fence ahead. From here make for the footpath sign to your right in the facing hedge. Cross the stile here and keep ahead beside the fence over this long field, which terminates as you climb up to negotiate another stile and turn right.

Go down the side of this field to a copse of silver birch, at the far side of which is a stile onto a rough road. Here you join the Sandstone Trail and turn right, ignoring the turn to Rawhead Farm as you continue ahead down a loamy path of soft earth. A crisscross stile takes you into a Wildlife Conservation Area and you soon reach a gently dripping rock overhang where a spring surfaces – known locally as the Droppingstone. Climb a set of sturdy

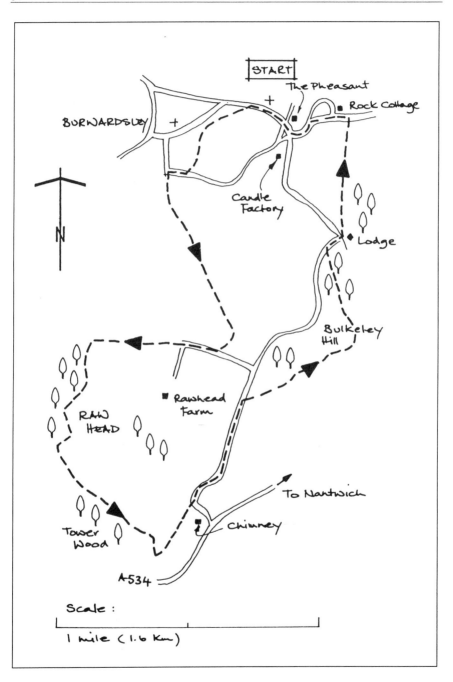

wooden steps to another stile, then pass a huge rock overhang on your way to a further one.

A scramble down below the path along here leads into a spectacular sandstone cave. Called the Queen's Parlour it is thought to have been made by local men excavating for sand. However, your route is above it along the top path, edging between the scarp and a field fence to the trig point at Rawhead – highest point of the Sandstone Trail (746 feet above sea level). From here you get outstanding views over the Cheshire Plain's patchwork of fields and woodland, as far as the misty outline of the Welsh hills.

Continue along the top of the cliffs, eventually descending rough-hewn steps in the rock, then work your way round the head of a deep gully, known as Musket's Hole. As you look back, the honeycombing effect caused by wind erosion is very evident on the rocky layers of this huge bastion of sandstone.

From here the path follows the edge of Tower Wood until you reach a signpost and turn left. Keeping along the fence and negotiating the aptly-named squeezer stiles, you soon drop downhill to cross a stream and follow the fence up to the end of the Wildlife Conservation Area. Notice the caves set back into the hillside here; in times past many of these were used as hide-outs for highwaymen accosting travellers on the road below.

Before turning left up the road glance down the field to where a solitary chimney still stands, relic of the pumping house which formed an essential part of the copper mine here in the 18th century. Then continue up the winding road until you negotiate a stile on the right between two gates, walk through a cattle pound and continue along the fence to the thickly wooded slopes of Bulkeley Hill.

Squeeze out of the field between posts, then climb through the wood, passing service huts for underground reservoirs deep below, before walking between iron gateposts. On this hill, rainwater percolates through porous sandstone. Collecting in natural water tanks when it reaches a layer of non-porous clay deep underground, this source provides enough water for the villages of south-west Cheshire.

Keep along near the top of the hill past an improvised trapeze dangling from the sturdy branches of a sweet chestnut. As you walk through a glade the winding branches of these trees are ideal for climbing, whilst the chestnuts, once devoid of their prickly shell and tough skin, provide a tasty snack – though they are better taken home and roasted in the oven.

Dropping steeply down the side of the hill to your right is a narrow, one-track tramway, built to transport heavy materials when a water pipeline was put in to tap the hilltop reservoirs. Your way, however, continues forward as chestnuts intermingle with oak and silver birch, and views over Peckforton Mere and the north-east open up through the trees. It is a good way before the path starts to drop down between bilberry and bracken to rough hewn steps, descending to a dirt track where you turn right.

At the lodge – the private entrance to the Peckforton estate – go left, and immediately right over a stile to follow the dry stone wall, bordering woodland, along a field's side. After crossing a stile and a second field, a further stile leads you to a fenced path, where another stile takes you into a dark passageway created by overhanging hollies. Follow the edge of a field and climb over a stile onto a road, where you turn left and pass pretty Rock Cottage before dropping down the hill back to The Pheasant.

South Cheshire

Audlem	Audlem SJ 64/74
Barthomley	Crewe SJ 65/75
Barton	Farndon, Holt & Tattenhall SJ 45/55
Tushingham	Whitchurch & Malpas SJ 44/54
Wybunbury	Crewe SJ 65/75 and Audlem SJ 64/74

The pubs in this area are full of both character and charm, each having an individuality of its own, and this is echoed in the walks too. You can walk along one of the prettiest sections of the Sandstone Trail, or have an awesome view of Wybunbury's famous leaning tower, then for water lovers, there are reed-fringed pools, canals and a water mill. Not an area endowed with stately homes, there are, nevertheless, several places worth a visit.

Stretton Mill

A visit to Stretton Mill can so easily be combined with the Barton Walk as you pass it 'en route'. The mill is now fully restored as a working water mill, where you can see the grinding of grain using millstones driven by a huge water wheel, and the stable block has displays telling the story of both mill and millers from its early days.

Follow the travel directions for the Barton Walk. The mill is open every afternoon except Mondays from March to October.

Telephone: Northwich (01606) 41331/40394 (Cheshire Museums).

Stapeley Water Gardens

Europe's largest water garden centre; fountains, pools and waterfalls abound, providing ideal habitats for a multitude of water plants and fish. Here too is The Palms, an unusual tropical oasis housing exotic hot-house plants, brightly coloured birds and exotic fish.

Take the A51 south-west from Nantwich and you soon reach Stapeley Water Gardens on the right; it is open all day every day. (Telephone: Nantwich (01270) 623868. Further along this road is the Wild Boar, starting point for the Wybunbury Walk.

Stretton Mill stands in picturesque surroundings. *(Photo: Cheshire Life)*

Bridgemere Garden World

This is the largest garden centre in the country, sited on the A51 south-east of Nantwich. It is open daily and has free entry and car parking. Telephone: Bridgemere (0193 65) 381.

Dorfold Hall

This Elizabethan hall, with its cobbled forecourt and avenue of ancient limes, can be found at Acton, near Nantwich. It is open to the public on Tuesday afternoons between April and October. Tel: (01270) 625245.

Cholmondeley Castle Gardens

Cholmondeley is a 19th century castle surrounded by attractive gardens, its grounds fanning out over the surrounding hillside. The gardens and grounds are open to the public on Sundays and Bank Holiday afternoons between Easter and September. Telephone: Cholmondeley (01829) 22383.

Audlem

Route: Audlem – Bennett's Bridge – A529 – Mill Lane – Audlem – Bagley Lane – Shropshire Union Canal

Distance: 6 miles

Start: Free car park in Audlem village or the large car park behind the Shroppie Fly. (SJ 658435)

By Car: Take the A529 south from Nantwich which passes through Audlem where a car park and toilets are on the right. Alternatively, you turn right to the Shroppie Fly before crossing the canal.

The Shroppie Fly – 01270 811772 (Free House)

This is one of five pubs in the little village of Audlem, so one is really spoilt for choice. Unique and off the road, the Shroppie Fly was once the granary warehouse for Kingbur Mill next door – now a canal shop. It was only converted to a pub 25 years ago – the brainwave of one Tim Hayward. The bar is made out of the original Shroppie Fly – a working barge carrying grain along the canal. One of the walls had to be knocked down to accommodate it, and its shining wood, topped by a miscellany of bottles and sparkling glasses, adds considerably to the unique atmosphere of the place, and on the cream-coated walls, are old canal scenes and a picture of Thomas Telford, designer of the canal.

At the height of the canal era fast fly-boats sped between Birmingham and Ellesmere Port and, to make the journey as fast as possible, they travelled through the night, illuminated by huge oil lamps. They could carry up to 25 tons of cargo, and typical goods would be: butter, cheese, ham and grain from the farming communities; coal, timber and limestone (for road building) from the industrial centres.

Each Saturday morning at one time a cheese boat sailed to Manchester from here, and the local farmers would cart their cheeses down to the canal for loading. Today, the front of the pub is dominated by an enormous crane – relic from the defunct railway nearby. This replaced the original canal crane, the base of which can still be seen embedded in the raised area where picnic tables now stand.

Nowadays, the canal is used only for leisure pursuits and, during the summer months, two travelling theatre companies perform traditional plays with a canal theme. One, the Daystar Theatre, performs off a barge that can often be seen moored further up the bank. There is also a raft race on the canal from Hankelow to Audlem in June, which attracts between thirty and forty rafts from all over the country.

The pub is particularly busy during the season, and at weekends throughout the year. The ample menu has around fifty meals on offer, everything from sandwiches and soups through to steaks, grills and homemade specials of the day.

Real Ale is served – Boddington's Bitter or Bass, Flowers, Wadsworths 6X with draught Guinness, cider, or low alcohol lager as alternatives. Included in the guide to 'Great British Pubs', the Shroppie Fly boasts visitors from as far afield as South Africa, New Zealand and America.

The Walk

Turn right along the tow-path, passing the lock-keeper's cottage. Off to the right is Moss Hall – an Elizabethan, timber-framed manor house dating from early in the 17th century; once a nunnery, there is reputed to be a tunnel joining it to the church. On the opposite bank an old stable block has been converted into a house, but it still bears a painted sign announcing that the stables are only to house the canal company's own animals. The dismantled railway runs away to your left, and you soon walk over the aqueduct high above the River Weaver, before leaving the towpath at Bridge 80 (Bennett's Bridge) through a steel gate.

Turn left here down a track that may leave you with mud-spattered boots, then turn right at a cross-tracks and almost immediately left over a stile. Keep ahead down the fence and cross two more stiles which take you onto a rough road. Then turn right, crossing the River Weaver at a picturesque, renovated mill, its old barn attractively converted into Riverside Mews. Mill House stands aloft as if guarding the privacy of this tiny community.

Carry on along the lane here to the main road, where you turn left for a short way towards Hankelow, then go right at a bend through a kissing gate. Keep the hedge on your right, walking towards the Parkes as you pass the massive bulk of Corbrook Court. Climb over a stile at the end of white fencing, where a welcome seat may afford you a few minutes' rest. Then continue down the road to a beech copse where you turn left.

Keep along this road, known as Monk's Lane, until you pass Mill House (with its faded sign), and turn right down the side of its double garage. The grassy track soon gives way to soft earth, and is still known locally as Mill Lane, although, as the path narrows to single file, a heap of mossy stones is all that now remains of the old mill. Keep left when you come to a rough track and drop down to the bowling green.

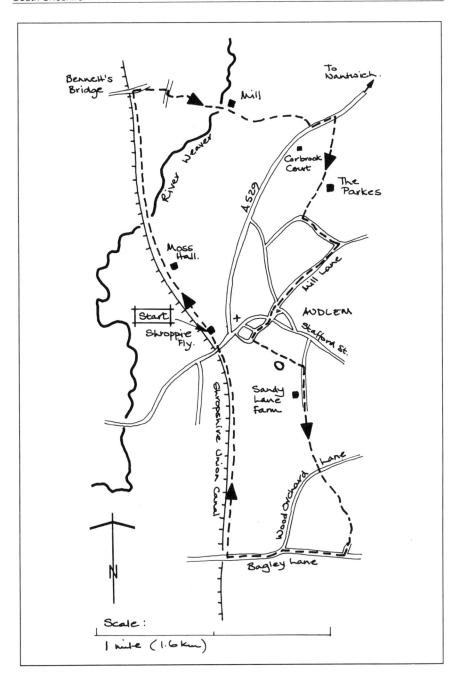

Bennett's Bridge

Mill

To Nantwich.

River Weaver

Corbrook Court

The Parkes

A 529

Moss Hall.

Mill Lane

Start

AUDLEM

Shroppie Fly.

Stafford St.

Sandy Lane Farm

Shropshire Union Canal

Wood Orchard Lane

Bagley Lane

N

Scale :
1 mile (1.6 km)

At Heathfield Road keep ahead to pass Taintree House on your way to Stafford Street, probably so named because it has always been the main road to Stafford from this area. Cross over, and keep ahead again down past Roseleigh and Brookside, where you bear left before passing Daisy Cottage. Leave the road at the old grammar school here, founded over 300 years ago by a Merchant Taylor of London, and now part of a housing development for the elderly. Then bear left over a hump-backed bridge.

Climb the stile here and keep ahead until the hedge ends; then continue forward past a pond to a stile in the field's far corner. Next, turn right down the lane, passing Sandy Lane Farm, then Field Farm, lying far over to your right as you continue ahead down a grassy track to Wood Orchard Lane.

Cross the stile in front of you here, and walk along the hedge for a short way until you strike out for the telegraph pole ahead. Next, make for the iron fence in the far left-hand corner, which gives access into the next field. Walk over this field to cross the wobbly stile at the far end, then pass a pond as you make for the gate in the right-hand corner.

Turn right, then right again at Bagley Lane, to pass Kinsey Heath Farm and a variety of cottages both old and new. Keep ahead as Wood Orchard Lane comes in from the right and, at Bridge House, go through a white gate and turn right along the Shropshire Union Canal. You pass most of Audlem's fifteen locks down here, their basins busy with boats in summer, in winter lined by hardy fishermen hoping to catch roach or dace. Built to facilitate the transport of goods between major cities such as Birmingham and London, Chester and Liverpool, this section was opened in 1835, and the locks here take the canal down from Shropshire to the Cheshire Plain – a descent of 93 feet.

The lock-keepers' huts often show the architecture of the age in miniature; some even have red brick walls, a slate roof and a chimney stack. Sheltered by high banks and hedgerows this is a pleasant part of the walk, and you soon pass under Grey's Bridge and arrive back in Audlem. After welcome refreshment at the Shroppie Fly, or one of the other four pubs in the village, you may wish to visit the church, or wander round the quaint village streets, often separated by narrow snickets.

Audlem

High above the heart of the village stands the Gothic church of St. James, which is well worth closer inspection. A scratch dial on one of the buttresses dates from medieval days, and the 14th century porch has sandstone seats worn smooth with much use. Inside, there is a fine oak ceiling and a Flemish chandelier. Iron bars in the chancel were erected in 1777 af-

The ancient buttermarket in Audlem dates back to the 18th century

ter an earthquake had severely shaken the church. During the last century, John Ellerton, writer of the hymn 'The day Thou gavest Lord is ended', preached from the fine old pulpit.

Outside the churchyard stands a pillared buttermarket, built in 1733, when a weekly market took place in the square. Beside it is a 'bear stone', to which a bear was chained, whilst men paid fees for their dogs to bait it. In the centre of the square is a memorial to a much-respected doctor who practised in the village for forty years during the 19th century, and on the corner stands the Crown Hotel – once a busy coaching inn.

Barthomley

Route: Barthomley church – Mill Dale – Lime Farm – Town House Farm – Mill Lane

Distance: 5 miles

Start: The White Lion. Take care with parking here. Stop beside the church wall or ask to use the pub car park.

By Car: Take the A5020 east from Crewe, continuing along the A500 to the roundabout at junction 16 of the M6. Turn sharp left here, signposted Alsager and Radway Green. Then take the next left turn down to Barthomley.

The White Lion – 01270 882242 (Burtonwood)

Barthomley lies tucked away amid precious green fields which still separate Crewe from the M6, a tiny hamlet that has changed little in the last 100 years. In the shadow of the ancient church of St Bertoline, the White Lion dates from 1614 when it was the clerk's cottage. Local records show that the parish clerks sold ale from here as early as the 16th century. For 200 years it was also the place where the Court Leet for the manors of Barthomley, Crewe Green and Leighton sat to dispense justice. Its name was derived from the family emblem of Sir Ranulph Crewe which depicted a silver lion.

In 1990 Terry Cartwright succeeded Mr Critchlow, landlord here for over forty years who, the locals will still tell you, was the youngest landlord in Britain when he took over on his 21st birthday. In Winter you can warm your cockles by two blazing, open fires, or a stove in the tiny backroom.

Open all day every day except Thursday, it only serves food, however, from noon to 2pm. All the dishes are home-made and probably the most reasonably priced of any Cheshire hostelry. The menu, displayed on blackboards, is changed daily and, in addition to a roast dinner, there may be hotte porke baton, hotte beefe banjo, hotte lambe torpedo or a cheese and onion oatcake. No sweets are served — a bonus for those on a diet! A function room can seat twenty or so to enjoy a buffet.

The beers are all Real Ale and include Top Hat and a guest beer which changes each month — probably one reason why The White Lion has always been a favourite with locals, ramblers and many others, who all enjoy soaking up the convivial atmosphere of this idyllic country inn.

St Bertoline

The ancient church of St Bertoline looms over the small car park – the only church in England to be dedicated to this 8th century prince, who became a hermit after the untimely death of his beautiful young wife.

The crenellated western tower with its eight pinnacles and grim faces dates from the 15th century. The church was the centre of a gruesome event in Civil War days when a Royalist raiding party rode into the village on Christmas Eve, 1643. These men, bent on rape and pillage, smoked out about twenty armed villagers, led by the Puritan schoolmaster, who had sought refuge in the tower, then stripped and shot twelve of them. Homes were looted, livestock killed, women raped. The sense of horror still remains.

Other items of historical interest include the Norman north doorway with its semi-circular arch, the arms of the Chester diocese and the Crewe family carved above the relatively new east window, and the 16th century rood-screen depicting Christ's birth and the Flight into Egypt. A walk round the churchyard reveals the recumbent effigy and tomb of Sir Robert de Foulshurst, decorated with weepers and dating back to 1390.

Thatched and half-timbered, the White Lion at Barthomley was once the parish clerk's cottage. *(Photo: Cheshire Life)*

The Walk

From the pub take the road towards Weston and Betley but immediately turn left at the parish notice board. Walk up to the village hall and continue up an almost hidden path. When the vicarage was built this pleasant diversion replaced the original right-of-way which bisected the house. (Even Vicars need some privacy!) Pass a pond in the copse before going over a stile into a field.

Cross a second stile, then head straight across the field, passing a pond in the dip on your left before topping a rise and making for a stile in the facing hedge. Keep ahead again (on rising ground) to another stile by a gate gap, then go forward once more to a stile in the corner of the facing fence. Continue in the same direction beside a hawthorn hedge as trim as boxed privet, before climbing rough-hewn steps to a stile which takes you, albeit briefly, into Staffordshire.

Turn right to another stile, then bear left to the hilltop and across to a stile in the fence on the right. Drop down the next field to a stile, below which a pretty fishing pool forms an idyllic picnic spot — backed seats even adding a touch of unexpected luxury! **Do not** climb over this stile, however, but turn right to follow the field's fringe, with Dean Brook meandering along the valley bottom.

Cross a dried up tributary, after which a stile takes you back into Cheshire. Keep ahead again at the next stile then, after a stile by a holly bush, stay above the stream, passing through a gap and continuing to the right of telegraph poles to a stile which leads onto a country lane. (Ignore the stile over to the right.)

Turn right here, passing the drive to Limes Farm then, after a short distance, turn left into a copse. After completing a dog-leg over two bridges, cross the huge field ahead, keeping a pond on your left. At its far side, continue into the next field over a hidden, corner stile (beyond a gateway). Bear right down the hedge, then left along a country lane.

You soon turn right over a stile and cross the field towards Town House Farm, where, adjacent to the stony farm track, is another stile. Cross the next field diagonally to a stile in the corner by a barn and, after negotiating a further stile, bear left along the hedge.

From here, Barthomley Church tower peeps out from the trees, its jagged battlements festooned with gruesome gargoyles and flying buttresses as it stands sentinel above Old Hall Farm, and you may hear the chimes of the church clock ringing out over the countryside. The original time-piece,

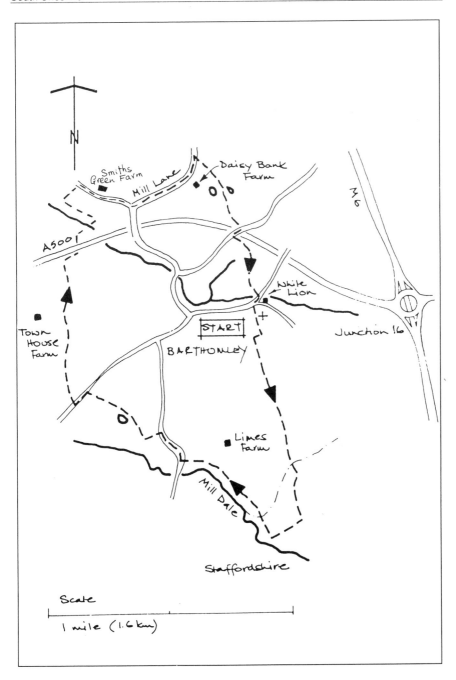

Smiths Green Farm

Daisy Bank Farm

Mill Lane

M6

A5001

White Lion

Town House Farm

START

BARTHOMLEY

Junction 16

Limes Farm

Mill Dale

Staffordshire

Scale

1 mile (1.6 km)

made by the village blacksmith in 1715, kept perfect time for 219 years before having to be replaced.

Cross two more stiles, then a hummocky field, after which you drop down a further meadow to stiles hidden behind an oak. In the following field, keep forward to a facing stile, walk alongside the wood to a stile behind a bramble patch, then up and onwards to a stile onto the A500. Cross this with care, bear right up the opposite bank to a stile, then continue up the field, dodging rabbit holes, until you finally drop down to cross a stream on an ivy-clad, brick bridge.

From here, bear left beside the stream and above the green-filmed, ox-bow lake cut off long ago. Continue along the hedge on the right and negotiate three, iron, stepladder stiles painted green. Next, turn right down the country lane, passing Smiths Green Farm on the way to a junction, where you turn left up Mill Lane, signposted Oakhanger.

After passing Daisy Bank Farm the M6 comes into view as you turn right over a stile. Walk beside the fence to a second stile, then a third, after which you skirt a pond before reaching a further stile between two gates. Continue along the track here, then over a stile beside a steel gate. Turn right at the track's terminus and cross the A500, again with care, before turning left at the top of the opposite bank to walk parallel with the road.

After a stile veer right towards the church and a stile beside a lone oak. Then head for the church again until you reach another stile — beside a gate and behind an upturned, old bath. A further stile (beside a water trough) takes you down a path between a barn and holly hedge, after which you keep ahead, then turn right beside black-and-white, beamed Bank Cottage into Barthomley village. Finally, don't miss the lichen-coated trough set in mellowed brick as you drop down to enjoy a welcome rest and refreshment at The White Lion.

Barton

Route: Cock o'Barton – Stretton Mill – Clutton – Coddington – Barton

Distance: Five miles

Start: Cock o'Barton (SJ 448541)

By Car: From Chester take the B5130 to Farndon where you turn left along the A534, following the line of an old salt route as far as Barton village. The pub is on your right at the crossroads and has a large car park behind it. (Please check with the landlord before abandoning your car.)

Barton Village

Standing 115 feet above sea level, the village of Barton dates as far back as Saxon times. Predominantly a farming community, it once had a much larger population, and a small quarry to the north down the old road once provided alternative employment for some of the villagers. The name of the hamlet was derived from the owners of the estate, the de Barton family, and the effigy of Patrick de Barton can be found in nearby Farndon church. Both the farmhouses in the village, and several of the old cottages, are listed buildings, as is the pub and its adjoining stables, which once provided shelter for eight horses.

Cock o' Barton – 01829 782277 (Free House)

Dating from the 14th century this grand old English pub – every building of note in Chester visible from its roof – was originally a posting house and coaching inn on the main route from Chester to Shrewsbury. In fact, although it is now located in Cheshire it still has a Shrewsbury post code. 'Shows how far behind the Post Office is,' was the landlord's caustic comment. Unlike many present-day landlords, John Hair has been at The Cock for twenty-five years and is justifiably proud of the fact, adding his own aura of stability to this solid building steeped in history.

The name, 'Cock o' Barton', was derived from the cock fighting pit nearby, where, legend says, passengers alighting from stage coaches were entertained whilst awaiting their meal. Grade 2 listed, parts of the building's fabric are 600 years old and the oak beams beside the fireplace at the east end are original. Alterations have been made to the structure every hundred years or so, the latest being the stone pillars added by the present landlord in the 1960s. Inevitably with a building of this antiquity, it is said to be haunted – by a male ghost, seen by the cook as he roams around the cellars and store room.

Mr John Hair, licensee, and regulars at the Cock o' Barton *(Photo: Cheshire Life)*

Always an independent Free House, three log fires warm customers on the coldest of days, the feeling of well-being perhaps enhanced by a pint of traditional beer or the mellow taste of one of the 200 brands of malt whisky on offer! (While waiting at the bar to be served pause to admire the picture of the window in Farndon Church which depicts the Civil War.) A large range of tasty food is served both at lunchtime and in the evening on every day except Monday. The menu is changed every month and there is always a selection of mouth-watering homemade deserts.

The Walk

Set off down the Roman road that stretches south from The Cock to Stretton, the massive bulk of Beeston Castle clearly visible on the skyline. After passing Stretton Lower Hall turn left to 18th century Stretton Mill. Here Carden Brook widens to make a mill pool with a picturesque, picnic spot, and ancient cobbles still front the slate-roofed buildings of stone and wood. The whole has been pleasingly restored, the wooden mill machinery, now in working order, being the oldest in Cheshire. Both mill and stable block are open each spring and summer afternoon.

Continue down the road past a wood and an impressive stone lodge, its 'stucco' pillars relics of past glory. The small plant nursery returns you to

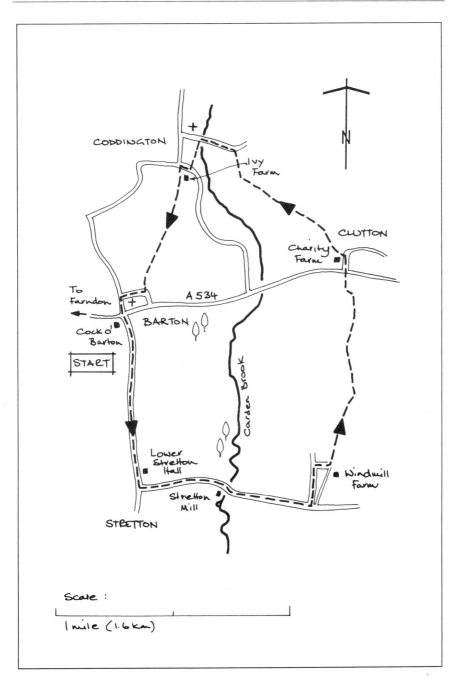

the present. Here turn left down the footpath to Clutton, passing Windmill
Farm. The track is bordered by solid, dry-stone walls of red sandstone, superb examples of a declining art. The wall continues to an oak-strewn parkland. Keep in the same direction and peer through a high iron fence at the
bowl-shaped Cheshire Plain rimmed by the misty outline of Welsh hills.
Turn right by a beech tree, perfect for climbing and, as usual, out of reach!

Soon you go left through a high gate to walk under overhanging outcrops of
ruddy sandstone, their surface ridged and furrowed by erosion, streaks of
white lime offering a sharp contrast. Patches of scrubby gorse flank the
path and Barton can be seen on rising ground above a silent lake. The grassy
path continues between grey boles of beech until you bear left through a
high steel gate. Here, turn right along a track flanked by hawthorn to the
A534 and the relic of an old weathered cross – a plaque denoting an award
for modern housing incongruously embedded in its well-worn surface.

Keep ahead down Holywell Lane passing Clutton general store, then turn
left down the drive in front of Charity Farm. This building dates from 1560,
its black and white 'magpie' walls haphazardly askew atop their stone base.
Climb over two stiles to enter a large field, and keep veering right down to a
line of oaks, where a bridge crosses a deep ditch into the next field. Follow
the hedge up this meadow, passing a circular water trough and then a small
pond before rounding the corner of the hedge; then turn right along a
cart-track (of sorts), which swings left by a reedy pond. Leave the track at its
end and cross the grass to the footpath sign in the fence.

Turn left along the lane, cross the stone bridge, then turn left at the footpath
before Coddington church. The old school beside it, enlarged in memory of
a local man, one Richard Massey who died in 1887, now acts as the village
hall. Pass to the left of the ancient tumulus. Rabbits pockmark the sandy
slopes which rise, encircled by hawthorn and surmounted by spruce. Walk
across to the gate in front of a farm, then turn right along the lane to pass Ivy
Farm, the duckpond opposite offering a sheltered habitat for mallards,
their well-adapted feet providing rapid propulsion over the murky surface.

Turn left down the footpath to Barton, keeping ahead at the farmyard entrance down a garden, dank and drenched in wintry weather but in Spring
splashed with the scarlet, yellow and blue of primula, daffodil and grape
hyacinth. Moss-covered stones point you down a path to a stile. You then
keep left down the field to another. Bear slightly right over the next field,
crossing the fence and making for the corner of a wood. Here, negotiate the
miscellany of stiles in the hedge beside a tower, then keep ahead down a
further field to a wide stile, and ahead again to a roadway. Turn right to
pass a milestone, dated 1898, then an old congregational chapel, built in
1877, before the road bears left and The Cock is ahead.

Tushingham

Route: Quoisley Bridge – Willey Moor Lock – Old Chad – Bradley Green – A41 – Jackson's Bridge – Shropshire Union Canal

Distance: 7 miles

Start: Quoisley Bridge (SJ 539462)

By Car: Take the A49 north from Whitchurch for about 2.5 miles. Park in a lay-by on the right, opposite Quoisley Lock.

Willey Moor Lock Tavern – 01948 663274

This pleasant and unusual Free House, with its array of Toby jugs (Charlie Chaplin is but one) and gleaming horse brasses, is well worth a visit, whether for a quick drink (coffee is always served) or a substantial meal.

The building dates from 1700 when it was a lock-keeper's cottage. Constructed on an oak raft, it flooded when the lock was first used. The original cottage was three up, three down, but has now been extended on both sides. At first the lock-keeper began to provide teas as a sideline, then ex-

Willey Moor Lock Tavern was originally the lock-keeper's home.
(Photo: Cheshire Life)

'Old Chad' – a church amid meadows. *(Photo: Cheshire Life)*

panded into serving drinks with meals. Ten years ago the present owner went to court and was granted a full licence (although there is no cellar) and use of a footbridge over the canal to give easy access from the car park. It is an unusual situation as the pub is in one district, the car park in another. The pub has had problems from inconsiderate walkers parking their cars and not actually patronising the pub. The gates to this car park are only open during business hours 12noon-2.30pm in winter, 12noon-3pm in summer and from 6pm in the evening, 7pm on Sundays. Any parking outside those times is prohibited.

Full meals are served at lunchtime and in the evening and the pleasant shaded garden and tables by the lock give this inn an idyllic setting.

The Walk

Cross the canal at Quoisley Bridge, drop down onto the towpath and turn right for the Sandstone Trail. At Willey Moor Lock Tavern walk past the old stables festooned with horseshoes – relics of earlier days when barges on the canal were horse-drawn. Continue in the front of the pub, then turn right alongside the garden, joining the Sandstone Trail to Bickley Wood.

Keep ahead, passing Moorhead Farm on your right and, after crossing the stile out of the next field, turn left then right. Here you may see rabbits, their white scuts bobbing, leap for cover into the base of a tree. Bear left round the next field, the lush meadows providing excellent grazing for dairy cattle. You soon see the signpost in the far hedge, where you exit and cross the lane which leads to Pearl Farm. Then climb the stile opposite, bearing left over the field, then right along a cart-track.

Cross the stile ahead and climb the hill in the dip between two telegraph poles, passing a key-laden ash before crossing the stile out of the field. Climb the slope across the next field, cross a stile and turn aside to visit St. Chad's church, where a proud weathercock struts atop the grey slates of the brick-walled tower and, in the words of a former vicar,

'It seems a place where time stands still, A place where one may know God's will.'

Although a chapel stood on the site long before 1690, the rebuilding of the present church took place then, and was paid for by a local lad, John Dod, who became a prosperous mercer in London. The gallery at the back was added later and can only be reached by stone steps outside. The church is still used for worship during the summer months, and a special rush-bearing service is held there in August.

There is no light and heat but the Vicar's seat used to have a container beneath it for hot coals, and all the furniture is of good quality Cheshire oak. The stump of a tree supports part of the pulpit, and also forms a seat for the reader of the lessons, and the font's pedestal may well have started off as the leg of a four-poster bed! It too is of oak, the intricate carving probably the work of a local craftsman.

It is tempting to linger in the quiet churchyard, shaded by massive yews and hollies, where rabbits share the sweeping views across the Cheshire plain. This is still the burial ground for the parish, the oldest visible grave being that of a monk. It is also worth a peek through the window of the small building (once used as the parish room) in the corner of the church-yard. Through this can be seen the original, horse-drawn parish hearse, built in 1880 and immaculately preserved.

As you leave this peaceful place the stile is in the middle of the far hedge. Then keep right until, after crossing another stile, you turn right again to skirt a field of nettles grazed by a flock of sheep. This is part of Barhill Development Farm, which tests animal foodstuffs, and also has several herds of cattle in the other fields surrounding its immaculate buildings. At the farmhouse turn left along the farm road to the A41, enjoying a view of the newer St Chad (completed in 1863) a church more accessible to the parishioners even if it lacks the quaint charm of the older, much-loved building.

Turn right for a short way along the A41, then left to Bradley (pronounced 'Bradeley'). After passing Parkers Well, Bradley Farm and Brook House you eventually reach the tiny Methodist church with the inscription 'Poor Man's Bethel' over the door. Look out for foxes in this area. You may see one ambling unconcernedly across the dismantled railway line, before you turn left down the almost hidden steps off the bridge. Princess Anne frequently hunts in this area, and it is also an excellent spot for blackberrying in September. Named Bradley Common, it is still preserved as common land, where anyone is allowed to graze three animals free of charge.

A forlorn sign in a garden states 'Beware of Trains. Look both up and down the line before you cross.' No need to do that nowadays! This line was one of the Beeching closures in 1956, after which each farmer bought pieces of it, using the embankments to store silage in black bags. Pass two houses before going through a gate in the hedge and crossing the field. Bear right past a solitary, wind-bent tree, then walk under the eerily echoing railway bridge.

Climb over the facing gate here and turn right in the field. The track rises to a clump of trees and a dried-up pond before you go through the gate into the next field. From here, keep left and then ahead through a grey, steel gate beside a water jump – one of the many different varieties of jumps in the

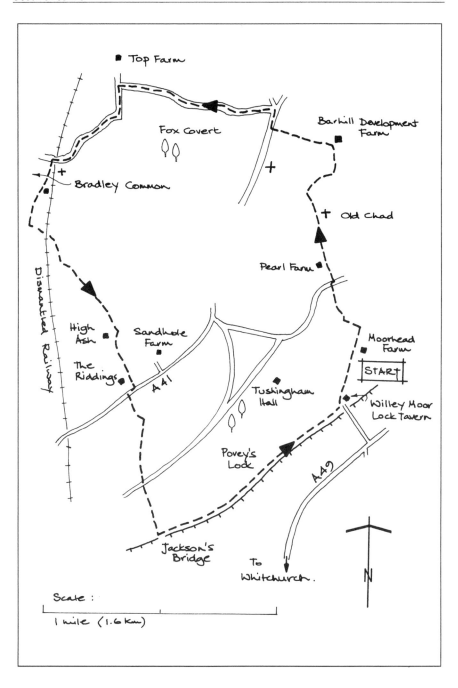

Scale :

|⊢————————————————⊣|

1 mile (1.6 Km)

fences here. Keep ahead down the left side of this field until you reach a stile. Pass the end of a copse of spruce and fir and continue forward. After walking behind a corrugated iron hut turn right to cross a private road and a stile.

From here, bear left and walk diagonally down the next two fields, making for The Riddings and a stile by an oak. Walk behind a large, grey hut and follow the hedge down to the A41, which you cross and turn right. Next, turn left over a stile, waymarked to the Sandstone Trail and Whitchurch

Keep to the side of the field, at the end of which is another stile which takes you ahead again to yet another stile. From here follow the stream down to cross a minor road, then continue towards the Sandstone Trail and Whitchurch over another stile. Bear diagonally right across this field to cross the stream where it disappears underground (at the first pylon). You then continue down the field until you go through a gate on your right. Keep forward again to the bridge over the canal ahead – Jackson's Bridge. After crossing a stile out of the field turn left along the towpath, signposted Willey Moor Lock and Bickley Wood.

What could be a more pleasant end to a walk than a grassy towpath surrounded by dairy herds and cornfields, the rustling of reeds along the banks as boats chug leisurely past, blue sky and fleecy clouds, butterflies and birdsong, and hedges of hawthorn and blackberry. The canal narrows considerably as you walk past Povey's Lock, and perhaps your footsteps quicken at the thought of a refreshing pint and a satisfying meal at the tavern ahead!

Wybunbury

Route: Walgherton – St. Chad's church – Wybunbury Moss – Wybunbury Tower – The Delves School

Distance: 3.5 miles

Start: The Boar's Head (SJ 698489)

By Car: The Boar's Head, on the outskirts of Walgherton, is on the busy A51 about four miles south-east of Nantwich.

The Boar's Head – 01270 841254 (Greenall Whitley)

Situated opposite the lodge gates of Doddington Hall, the gardens of which were designed by Capability Brown, the Boar's Head dates back to 1634. Once a coaching inn, some of the buildings associated with this are still standing. An old inventory hanging inside lists stables and stalls, trap house, loose boxes, shippon and provender store; two piggeries, a fowl house and shed indicate that the publican produced *truly* homemade breakfasts for his guests.

The inn itself is attractive with its half-timbered gable. To add to the atmo-

The Boar's Head stands opposite the lodge gates of Doddington Hall

sphere of the place, strange happenings occur, such as keys disappearing then turning up in odd places. Locals think they are moved by a man who still returns to haunt the building, after being murdered in a pub brawl many years ago.

The Boar's Head serves Greenalls', Boddingtons and Bass beers. It has an extensive menu to suit most pockets and palates, and there are also 'specials' on every day.

The Walk

Leave the Boar's Head car park and turn right towards Nantwich, taking care as you walk along this busy road. You soon pass a lovely old cottage called Thatchers and turn through a gate. Then walk down the field towards Wybunbury Tower, the hedge first on your right, then your left as you cut into a second field. Keep on alongside the hedge as the track ends and at the end of the hedge, keep ahead to a stile. Drop down the field ahead, noticing the bungalows whose occupants once had smallholdings, referred to locally as 'wheelbarrow farmers'. When you reach the track, which is Sally Clark's Lane, turn left along it. According to records of 1851 (when she was 84) it was named after a pauper woman who lived there.

When you come to the second cattle grid look ahead to Brook House, noticing the quoins down its thick stone walls as you turn right through the gate into the field. Cross Checkley Brook before climbing up the hill to a hidden stile which takes you into the village playing fields.

You soon reach the modern St. Chad's church. Over the centuries five churches have collapsed on the higher ground where Wybunbury Tower now stands alone, the nature of the land there being very unstable. In the early 1970s, the decision was taken to build a modern church and vicarage here, which recently celebrated its tenth anniversary. For this occasion the Wybunbury Silver, normally locked in a bank vault, was on display. It was discovered in 1969 when Rev. Stanley Jones (Vicar at that time) decided to investigate the contents of an iron chest in the tower, thinking to throw away a hoard of accumulated junk. Instead, he unearthed seven valuable pieces of antique silver, including a chalice, flagon, spoon and lidded tankard, all probable relics from an earlier church.

From the church turn right along Main Street to see several of the older properties of the village, including Village Farm, now a modernised house but dating back 200 years. The post office used to belong to a well-known saddler called H.E. Bourne, and the village hall, at one time a National school for infants and older girls, is now well used by local societies. There

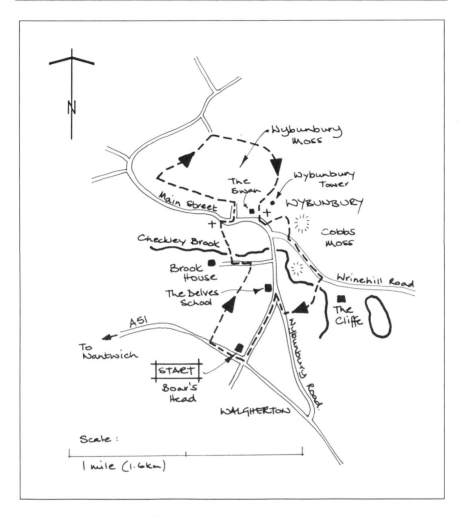

is an attractive row of Elizabethan cottages too, their gabled windows protruding quaintly from pointed eaves.

Turn left down Kiln Lane, so-called because a lady living here had a kiln in
her back garden. You get a glimpse of the Methodist church, built in 1864
and generously sharing its premises with the Anglicans while their present
church was built.

Ahead is Wybunbury Moss, a national Nature Reserve which scientists
consider to be one of the best examples of a floating bog in Western Europe.
It consists of forty feet of water underlying a raft of peat, only three feet deep

in places and covered by sphagnum moss. The pointed tops of Scots pine peep out above a mass of mixed woodland, consisting chiefly of silver birch, interspersed with a smattering of alder, oak and sallow, and a reed swamp edges the outer perimeter to form a creeping bog. Some trees are systematically culled as there are not enough nutrients to sustain them all.

Conservation groups regularly come to investigate the rare fauna and flora of this environmental miracle, and many rare insects make their home here. Of particular interest is a small spider, its first British sighting occurring here in 1963. Dead wood provides a comfortable home for a rare species of wood beetle. The tiny sundew plant can also be spotted, obtaining the food with which to sustain its life from minute spoonlike structures. Wild orchids, cows tongue and cranberries also thrive here.

At the end of the lane turn left over a stile to walk above The Moss, negotiating two more stiles before crossing a house drive and continuing down a snicket to a further stile. Keep in the same direction over another field, to a stile which brings you out onto a dirt lane, where you turn right and continue alongside The Moss itself. (While walking in this area it is exceedingly dangerous to venture off the path.)

You soon climb a stile onto a path that takes you behind a farm specialising in rare breeds of sheep and goats. The gingery goats originated from the Channel Islands, where all but two of the breed were killed for food during the Second World War– the last pair only surviving because they were hidden in a cellar. The goats' milk is exported from the milking parlour to delicatessens in Manchester and is recommended for sufferers of eczema. The tiny Soay sheep were salvaged from the Highlands of Scotland, where they too were almost extinct.

After passing hen huts, you reach a Water Board pumping station which houses a specially designed pump from Japan, its installation costing £80,000. It's hoped that it will succeed in pumping polluted water from the Moss back to the main sewers. Continue through a snicket, where wild rose grows through a hedge of bramble and broom, hawthorn and holly. It leads to a busy dairy – the attractive slate of house and wall imported from Cumbria.

As the tarmac road bears left you keep ahead over a stile, walking through two fields known locally as 'the rabbit fields'. It's easy to see why as you keep below the bank studded with bramble, hawthorn, glorious yellow gorse, elder, oak and holly. Walk through a gap in the facing hawthorn hedge and turn right through a small iron gate beside a sturdy fence – known locally as the Horse Leap. Keep along here until you cross a stream –

its milky water and nasty smell providing ample evidence of the Moss's pollution. Then climb uphill to the churchyard.

As you emerge from the lychgate look down the street to the Red Lion, once a coaching inn and now the meeting place for local fishermen and the darts team. The smithy used to be next door and the butcher's shop is still there. Both the Red Lion and the Swan date from the 18th century, and the latter offers accommodation as well as food and drink. The Elizabethan cottage adjoining it is the oldest house in the village. Originally built with no foundations, this has now been rectified, and the whole dwelling renovated in keeping with its original character.

At one time Figgy Pie Wakes used to take place here at Christmas; stalls were set up, and the villagers gambled to see who could roll figgy pies the furthest. However, rumour has it that this custom came to an abrupt end when Black Jack (a local ruffian) was killed in a drunken brawl.

You are now standing at the heart of one of Cheshire's oldest villages. Mentioned in the Domesday Book and lying amidst rolling countryside to the south of Crewe, Wybunbury's massive leaning tower stands in solitary state, an outstanding local landmark. Now classed as an ancient monument, it dates from the late 15th century, but there has been a church on this site since Norman times. A considerable amount of money has been spent on making its foundations safe and redressing its lean, which had reached four feet out of true.

Flying buttresses gaze down at the surrounding village, and the six bells now ring out again from their lofty belfry. Cast in the late 18th century, each bears an individual inscription and the rhyme,

'If for to ring you do come here, You must ring well with hand and ear; And if you ring in spur or hat, A quart of ale you pay for that; And if a bell you overthrow, Sixpence you pay before you go. These laws are old, they are not new, Therefore the clerk must have his due.'

As you pass the tower glance towards the lychgate, erected as a memorial to those who lost their lives in the First World War, then turn left to continue down through the cemetery. If you look back at the west door you will notice the raw redness of the sandstone. This was quarried in Runcorn, whereas the huge, older blocks at the other side of the building may have come from Delamere in much earlier times. The path here is formed by ancient gravestones and leads down to a small gate.

The house to your right was once the vicarage, its grounds providing an ideal venue for garden parties. The grassy area behind was occupied by the Vicar's cows and the fields ahead, separating Wybunbury from the neigh-

Wybunbury's famous leaning tower

bouring village of Hough, have always been known as The Lawns. Turn right along a track, pausing at a gate to look over to a clearly defined moated site. Wybunbury boasts two such sites. A safe house was built on this one after an early Bishop of Lichfield was mugged on his journey to Chester. On reaching Wrinehill Road – originally a turnpike road joining Nantwich and Newcastle-under-Lyne – turn left and you soon pass the other, earlier moated site, where a manor house known as The Flint More once stood.

Turn right down here towards Hough Mill Farm, crossing Checkley Brook – a tributary of the River Weaver. Keep your eyes open and, after the first fence, turn right again to climb over a stile and continue uphill. If you look into the trees to the west you may catch a glimpse of The Cliffe, a typical Cheshire 'magpie' building, and a maternity home until 1961. At the time of writing sand quarrying is much in evidence here, but the contours will eventually be restored to their original shape. A former sand quarry further down Wrinehill Road is now a large lake and home of Wybunbury Angling Club.

Turn right after crossing the stile onto Wybunbury Road, and you will soon reach a junction and be facing the Delves School. This was built in 1822 as a National School for Boys, and is now the local primary school – its modern extensions fanning out to the rear. If you face the original building, the left section used to be the school house.

To your right is Bridge Street, once called Grub Street, supposedly because a wood had to be 'grubbed' up to make way for it. At one time the rent for the old cottages down here used to be 3s 4d a week, and this princely sum also included rates. Number 23 was the last private school in the area, known as Mr Joynson's Academy. The present owner wondered why he kept finding so many flat pieces of slate in his back garden until he was given an old photograph of the school children in front of his porch. How forbidding the teacher looked, and how cross the little girl was at having to sit next to her male counterpart! And how many small children must have practised the Three Rs on those slates.

Down here too, on the road back to the village centre, is Brook Bridge, stoically suffering the surfeit of juggernauts 'en route' to the M6. However, you are going to turn left towards Walgherton and a welcome at the Boar's Head.

Later, warmed and rested, you might get a final glimpse of Wybunbury Tower as it glows warmly in the lamplight, fading with Wybunbury Moss into the eerie mist of early darkness. The village people have had to fight to keep these two phenomena: one historical, the other natural – but both now assured a lasting place in our fragile English heritage.

North-East Cheshire

Alderley Edge	Macclesfield & Alderley Edge SJ 87/97
Little Bollington	Warrington SJ 68/78
Ollerton	Northwich & Knutsford SJ 67/77
Rostherne	Warrington SJ 68/78
Styal	Stockport (South) SJ 88/98

Dunham Massey

A Georgian mansion, incorporating a fine collection of furniture, paintings and Huguenot silver. The Little Bollington Walk passes through the 250-acre deer park which surrounds it, where fallow deer wander unconcernedly through the trees.

Take Junction 7 off the M56 towards Altrincham. Turn left at traffic lights onto the B5160 (Charcoal Road) and you eventually reach the estate car park on your left. It is open every afternoon between April and October except Friday. Telephone: Altrincham (0161) 941 1025.

Tatton Park

The former home of the Egerton family, Tatton Park was left to the National Trust in 1958. The impressive 18th century hall, with its splendid, pillared portico, houses a large collection of the family's pictures, furniture, glass and silver. In the tenants' hall, African trophies leer from the walls, and entertainments are put on throughout the year. Outside is a white, marble statue of Charlotte Egerton, drowned in Tatton Lake on the eve of her wedding, and the 50-acre garden includes an orangery and an authentic Japanese area complete with Shinto temple. The surrounding park, with its herds of red and fallow deer, extends over 1,000 acres and incorporates two meres, on the larger of which sailing is allowed, and a 1930s farm is another attraction.

Take the A50 from Knutsford and follow the signs to Tatton, which is open every afternoon from the beginning of April to the end of October. Telephone: Knutsford (01565) 654822.

Peover Hall Gardens

The Elizabethan brick manor house overlooks idyllic gardens with roses, herbs, topiary hedges and a lily pool, all enclosed by clipped yews and mellow brick walls. The gardens are open every Monday afternoon. Telephone: Lower Peover (01565) 812404.

Nether Alderley Mill

South of Alderley Edge on the A34, Nether Alderley is a restored 15th century overshot water mill, and is open on certain afternoons between April and October. Telephone: Alderley Edge (01625) 523012.

The 15th-century mill at Nether Alderley

Quarry Bank Mill

Now owned by the National Trust, this 'factory village' was set up in 1784 – the brainchild of Samuel Greg, a pioneer of the factory system, whose cotton cloth was sold all over the world. The Victorian iron water-wheel still stands at the centre of the mill which is now a working museum. Here, ex-mill hands can be seen operating a spinning jenny or a Crompton's mule, and visitors can experience the deafening noise of the weaving shed.

Nearby is the Apprentice House, where children, aged between seven and fifteen, were housed, clothed, fed and nursed when ill. The old village store and school can be seen, and the mill-workers' cottages, each with its strip of garden. The Styal Walk takes you past all these, plus the Norcliffe Unitarian Chapel, where the non-conformist Greg family worshipped each Sunday, and where many memorials are dedicated to them. It is open from 2.30 to 5pm each Sunday between Easter and September.

To reach Quarry Bank Mill follow the travel instructions for the Styal Walk. Apart from Mondays, it is open every day throughout the year. Telephone: Styal (01625) 527468.

Hare Hill Gardens

Take the B5087 between Alderley Edge and Prestbury to reach this walled garden with pergola and outstanding displays of rhododendrons and azaleas. It is open on certain afternoons between April and October. Telephone: Upton Magna (01743) 77649/77343 (National Trust).

Jodrell Bank

From every conceivable viewpoint looking out over the Cheshire Plain the unusual sight of Jodrell Bank's famous radio telescope, completed in 1957, can be seen. 250 feet in diameter, its giant saucer-shaped bowl scans the heavens, collecting valuable information for scientists and weathermen. There are interesting displays and space models in the adjacent buildings, and a planetarium gives shows at regular intervals during the day. On the site there is also an arboretum for those interested in trees and shrubs.

Take the A535 south from Alderley Edge, and Jodrell Bank is on the right. Open most days, telephone Lower Withington (01477) 71339 for details.

Alderley Edge

Route: Duke Street – The Edge – Clock House Farm – B5087 – White Barn Farm – Swiss Hill

Distance: 5.5 miles

Start: The Drum and Monkey (only if patronising the pub) (SJ 848787)

By Car: Take the A34 south from Wilmslow. In Alderley Edge turn sharp left off the railway bridge down Heyes Lane. After passing the Royal Oak look out for the right turn to the Drum and Monkey. (It is the turn before the triangle fronting Duke Street and Moss Lane.)

The Drum and Monkey – 01625 584747 (Robinson's)

For well over a hundred years, the Drum and Monkey has been hidden away at the far end of a row of cottages. With its immaculate bowling green lying in a lovely garden setting, it is well worth seeking out. For some years it was called the Moss Rose but it has now reverted to the Drum and Monkey – its original name – and there are two stories as to why it was so called. One is that an organ grinder used to frequent the bar with a monkey on his shoulder. The other concerns the railway which ran down from the Edge to offload ore nearby; the skip carrying the ore was the drum and the man who was the off-loader was the monkey.

Catering is available from noon to 2.30pm and 6pm to 9pm, Monday to Saturday. There is a full menu plus a 'specials' board. On Sundays a traditional roast meal is available from noon to 7pm. Book in advance for Sunday 'lunch' or for groups. E-mail to drumandmonkey@kalton.co.uk, phone as above or fax to 01625 584975.

The pub is open all day, every day, seven days a week. Walkers are always welcome but the licensee asks that you shouldn't leave your car in the car park if you are not going to patronise the pub as it does get very full.

The Walk

Walk back past the row of terraced cottages and turn right onto Heyes Lane, passing the grocers with its incredible selection of cheeses before turning right again down the cobbled surface of Duke Street. One of the properties along here has the brightest display of springtime primulas I have ever seen – the plants gigantic, the flowers a riot of brilliant colour.

Keep ahead down Marlborough Avenue into Moss Lane, and then cross the main road to Squirrel Bank, turning right and then left up Squirrel's Jump.

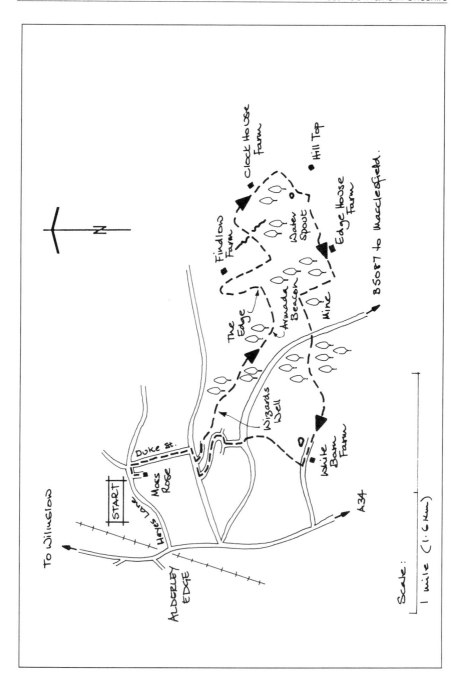

This leads you onto National Trust property, with good views of the fertile plain below and, as you climb gently up a leafy path, giant beeches tower up the steep bank. The Edge itself is 650 feet high and two miles long, its precipitous slopes covered mainly in beech and Scots pine.

Ascend by the steps when you reach them – more strenuous this! – and go left past Wizard's Well with its cryptic inscription: *'This water flows by the Wizard's will'*. Can you see the face above? Walk on alongside rock over-hangs, moss-covered and damp, to the viewpoint. Then keep along the top path, bearing right up more steps to Stormy Point where, in 1588, a beacon was lit to warn of the Spanish Armada's arrival.

When continuing from here, take the next path to the left from the one on which you arrived. This will take you down a dip and then up onto The Edge itself, starkly rising above the plain. All this land was a gift from the Pilkington family to the National Trust in 1948. Bear left at the Memorial Stone to the family, then meander down to the bottom path, turning right to the old railway line which exits from the fiery rock face known as Hough Level.

Keep left around the perimeter of the wood, circling Findlow Farm to the stream in its deep cleft. Cross this, then climb up the hill, where severely eroded rock overhangs are mantled by grass and moss in variegated greens. Bear left up here and keep left along a path, parts of which can be very muddy after a spell of wet weather.

You soon pass Clock House Farm, and leave the wood where a sign points left to Hare Hill. However, you turn right over a stile and walk down the fence with Hill Top over to your left. After passing a pond bear left and then right over another stile which leads to a gorse-flanked path. It is worth bear-ing right for a few paces after crossing the next stile to see the water spout pouring from its rocky lip. Then retrace your steps and turn right to Edge House Farm. Turn right again at the end of the hedge down a tiny path, and then go left, passing an oak tree and keeping ahead at the stile.

At the unsurfaced, stony road turn right, going through the fence and bear-ing sharp left past sheer, red-stoned cliffs. From here you eventually climb up to a disused mine – one of many in this area which is riddled with old workings; for copper and lead have been mined here since before Roman times. Turn right down the mine's near side and follow this direction to the National Trust donation box and a delightful stone cottage, its mullioned windows glinting in the sunlight below sheltering eaves. The initials JTS and MJS signify that it was built by Sir John Thomas Stanley and his wife, Maria Josepha, in 1837, to house estate workers.

Cross the busy road and go into the wood, darkened with evergreens, then lightened as shimmering sunlight dapples through the leafy branches of deciduous trees. Continue down here until you reach an open common, the sandy soil underfoot only supporting coarse grass interspersed with gorse, broom, and the spindly trunks of silver birch.

Bear right as you reach this area to a gate and a stile, where you keep ahead to pass between White Barn Farm and a still, clear lake. At the end of the drive turn right over a stile, then walk diagonally right across the field, following the fence to a stile in the far corner. From here, keep beside the brick wall to another stile, from which a dirt path, flanked by high holly hedges, takes you to the road.

Many of the large houses in this area were built in the middle of the last century when the railway company, keen for people to settle here and use the train to travel to work, offered a first class season ticket to Manchester for twenty years, to anyone who built their own house here.

Cross over this road and go down Underwood Road where, at the house named Franklyn, you bear right and then left down the flat, square cobbles of Swiss Hill. This is a cool ending to the walk on a hot day, the view over Alderley Sports Club showing off its ample facilities for cricket, hockey and tennis.

Turn right at the bottom of the hill and then left down Moss Lane, retracing your steps to the pub, perhaps to watch the bowls while enjoying a cool drink, or even a well-earned lunch.

Little Bollington

Route: Bridgewater Canal – Dunham Woodhouses – Agden Bridge – Ye Olde Number Three – Arthill Farm – Swan with Two Nicks – Dunham Massey

Distance: 6 miles

Start: Axe and Cleaver (SJ740881)

By Car: Take the A50 from Warrington towards Manchester, turning left at traffic lights onto the A56. Four miles the other side of Lymm turn left towards Altrincham at a roundabout. Then take the first left turn at traffic lights towards Dunham Massey, the second right through Dunham Town, and the right fork at the church. There is an ample car park behind the pub.

Axe and Cleaver – 0161 928 3391 (Chef & Brewer)

At one time a local man brewed beer in his cottage here, which gradually became the village's tavern where business was brisk. Much later, the Axe and Cleaver was established in its spacious and elegant mansion.

The 20th century lead to increased fortunes for The Axe and Cleaver, as the attractions of a public house in a picturesque setting increased custom.

The Axe and Cleaver's impressive façade. *(Photo: Cheshire Life)*

The pub has a daily choice of main courses, starters and puddings displayed on chalkboards as well as the "finest full-bodied ales". They also have a comprehensive restaurant menu from snacks through to full meals.

The Walk

Turn right down the road to the Bridgewater Canal, passing the old school dated 1759 and now used as the village hall. Cross Dunham School Bridge here before turning along the tow-path towards Lymm. Take care not to trip over iron mooring rings, where multi-coloured barges often share the banks with fishermen in silent contemplation, and solid balks of timber bide their time until needed for repairs.

Drop down off the canal path at the aqueduct and turn right along the road to Dunham Woodhouses – so named because the houses were built here on land cleared of woods and scrub in the late Middle Ages. Later, woodsmen working on the Dunham Massey estate occupied the pretty cottages. At a hairpin bend turn left down Meadow Lane, crossing the beck where sprays of wild rose and elder enhance the hedgerow. Continue up the hill to the stile by a telegraph pole. Then follow others which march across the next field to a stile and stream. After this, walk the plank in the middle of the field, and make for the mature ash tree ahead, from which you go forward again, before turning left at the field's end to a track. Then turn right and walk past Woolstencroft Farm to the road.

A left turn brings you to Agden Bridge, which you cross before going left again, and then taking the short cut down a 'No Through Road' to the A56. Here keep left again, crossing over to walk on the footpath towards Ye Olde Number Three – originally called the Red Lion. Some locals think its name was changed either because it was the third pub in Little Bollington to be built or because it is reputed to have three ghosts – all friendly. However, the most likely explanation stems from the last century when it was the third stop for a change of horses pulling fast passenger boats along the Bridgewater Canal between Chester and Manchester.

Turn right down the footpath immediately opposite the pub, walking down the first field before bearing left through a gate at the end. Continue in the same direction until you cross a stile into a further field, where the wood still shown on OS maps was totally uprooted in the 1960s. As you turn left along the tractor track to Arthill Farm market gardening is much in evidence and, in late summer, colourful crops of dahlias and chrysanthemums will be sold at Manchester's wholesale market. Pass the farmhouse and keep ahead between rows of glasshouses before continuing down a path bordered, in late summer, by pom-pom dahlias splashing the field with a profuse variety of vivid colour.

Cross the road and keep ahead past the sign 'Watch Out, Rottweilers About'

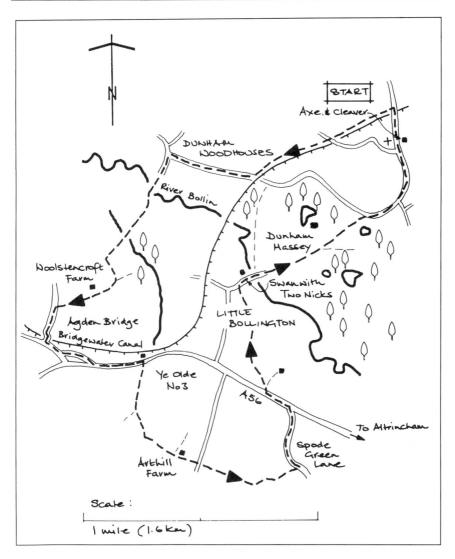

– with luck there will be no sign of them. Skirt the edge of the mixed wood ahead, where oak and silver birch mingle harmoniously with hawthorn and holly, and a flock of fat pigeons may whirr into the spring air with a ca-cophonous clamour of vigorously flapping wings. After passing a silent pond, bear left to cross an array of planks and drop down the field. Then turn left again over the fence, negotiate the gate on your left and continue down the track to another gate onto Spode Green Lane, where you turn left once more.

Turn left along the A56 where you have an uninterrupted view to Dunham Massey estate. This covers more than 200 acres and has ancient trees well past their bicentenary. You will soon spot an old, iron footpath sign in the hedge opposite, where you turn right for a short distance towards New Farm. Then turn left to Bollington at another signpost. Bear left over a stile into the next field alongside a hawthorn hedge, then cross two stiles separated by a muddy track. A further stile, quite hidden at the field's end, gives access to a hedge littered with brambles showing promise of an ample harvest to come.

Keep ahead along a short path until you reach The Swan with Two Nicks, its name referring to the nicking of a swan's beak to establish ownership. This pub is supposed to have been a popular 'watering' place for Dick Turpin on his sorties north. Although the once-rioting wisteria has given way to brightly coloured window boxes, the beer continues to be of good repute. Turn right here and cross the millrace, where the ex-flour mill's huge wheel once used water diverted from the Bollin. After modernisation, this wheel was said to be the best in Cheshire.

Keep ahead along the footpath here to Dunham Massey, negotiating the stepladder at Bollington Gate. Fallow deer mince unconcernedly among the trees as you pass a 16th century mill, its now-idle wheel still visible, and then bear left at the fork past the hall. One of the National Trust's historic houses, it incorporates fine furniture, impressive portraits and a dazzling collection of Huguenot silver. Adjacent to the path, Smithy Pool, abundant with ducks and geese, perhaps basks in soft spring sunshine as you continue through Smithy Gate.

Turn right here and immediately left down Woodhouse Lane to Dunham Town, where 18th century estate cottages border the road, both builder and date often signified in the mellow brickwork. Continue down School Lane, passing St. Mark's church, and the post office advertising old-fashioned, dairy ice cream, before reaching journey's end.

Ollerton

Route: Windmill Wood – Booth's Hall – Springwood Farm – Marthall Brook – Ollerton Farm

Distance: 4 miles

Start: Dun Cow (SJ 775769)

By Car: The Dun Cow stands on a bend, about 4 miles from Knutsford on the A537 – the main road to Macclesfield.

Dun Cow – 01565 633093 (Partition Newcastle)

Nowadays Ollerton is chiefly noted for its rose-growing nurseries and garden centres, but this was not always so. In the last century the Dun Cow was a court-house for petty sessions of the Bucklow Hundred; prisoners awaiting trial were chained to the cellar's wall and, if proved guilty, were beheaded in Knutsford. The lounge was the court-room, and the snug – the magistrate's retiring room.

Many of the original beams can still be seen. The solid, oak-beamed doorway is original too, and a framed tapestry in the lounge is a remnant of the

The Dun Cow was once the local court-house

first wall covering. In 1950 the bar was added, and the cellar was shored up to halt its collapse after being founded on shifting sand.

The pub serves food from noon until 2 pm and in the evening during the week, and all day at weekends. Its traditional Sunday lunch remains popular but there is also a full, alternative menu and a 'specials' board which changes daily. Home-made soup and sandwiches can be ordered in advance by any walking group and, for Real Ale buffs, the guest bitters vary from week to week.

The Walk

Walk along the road towards Knutsford, passing tree nurseries, then Ollerton Grange, the lodge and Kerfield House. On the edge of the wood opposite is a turnpike cottage, a reminder that from about 1795 onwards this was a turnpike road. After passing Manor Lane cross over and turn left into the wood after the bus-stop, walking down through this, and forking right where it opens out into glades of fern and rhododendron. Clumps of primroses bunch beneath towering beeches here.

Turn right when you meet a selection of tracks, then bear left along the edge of the wood. This takes you down an avenue of sleek, grey-boled beech trees, with an intermittent sprinkling of birch and oak, bramble and holly. On an Ordnance Survey map this is called Windmill Wood, but to the locals it is simply Toft Wood. From here the spire of Toft church stands above the fields; inside, the impressive font is carved with angels and vivid Bible scenes.

Turn right down Goughs Lane, which takes you back to the main road. Far to the left is the stone obelisk, probably built to commemorate a 14th century chapel, built by the Legh family as a place where Knutsford folk could worship and bury their dead. From here keep ahead down Booths Hall Drive, skirting Toft Cricket Club, where the boles of ancient oaks protrude from the twiggy entanglements of witches broom.

The original Booths Hall was built in the 14th century on the opposite side of the drive to the present building. Its half-timbered structure similar in design to Little Moreton Hall, it occupied the largest moated site in Cheshire. The gracious, Georgian building we see today replaced it in the 18th century, the same architect also designing Knutsford Parish Church. The crest of the Legh family is set into stonework on either side of the main doors and a sweeping staircase rises from the imposing entrance hall, its shallow steps only six inches high to accommodate crinoline-clad ladies! Another gracious room is the oak panelled lounge known as the Oak Room, where a bureau built into the wall facing the fireplace gives hidden access

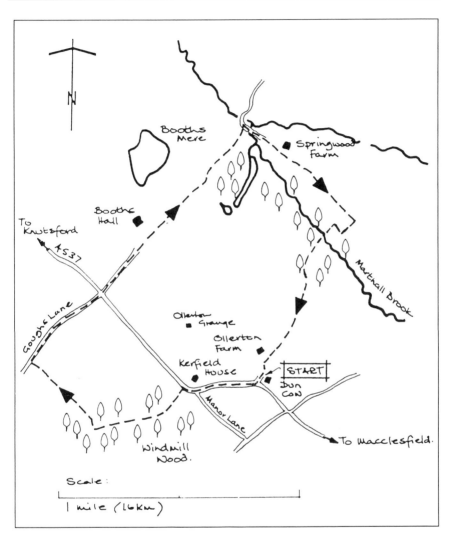

to the cellars. The ghost of a young maid-servant flitting through the rooms is said to add to the atmosphere.

Although the Nuclear Industry first leased the property in 1955, it was not actually purchased by NNC until 1981 and, although purpose-built offices and car parks have been built for the work-force, the ivy-covered old hall, plus the extensive parkland and meres, have been preserved to provide a very pleasant work-place.

As you pass Booths Hall farmhouse and outbuildings the road gives way to a cart-track. At the entrance to a drive turn left down a path. From here, go right over a fence, before walking alongside Spring Wood, which hides a pretty lake. Keep ahead again after passing through a red gate. Then drop down the track on your left and cross over a babbling brook to leave the field.

Next, turn right along a stony track, and walk ahead through the farmyard of Springwood Farm. Continue forward, with oak trees in the surrounding fields offering shelter from the weather to both birds and cows. Walk alongside the hedge now until, at the end of the fourth field, you reach a pond where you bear right. A wide view over the Pennines shows Shutlingsloe's prominent, cone-shaped peak and, farther south, the scarp and dip of Bosley Cloud.

When you reach a barbed wire fence turn right alongside it, which brings you down a spongy valley to a wood. Turn right beside this to a stile into it. Drop down to cross the bridge over Marthall Brook and continue ahead alongside its tributary until you leave the wood over a stile and planks.

Keep ahead all the way to Ollerton Manor, passing through a kissing gate on the way. Then turn left to walk alongside the tennis court before bearing right, then right again along a crunchy gravel track to a small gate at the manor's entrance. From here, keep ahead for a short distance until you turn left at the main road back to the Dun Cow.

Rostherne

Route: Chapel Lane – Booth Bank – A556 – Rostherne Mere – Tatton Dale –
Mere Farm – Bucklow Hill

Distance: 7 miles

Start: The Swan (SJ 731832)

By Car: Take the A50 from Knutsford towards Warrington. Turn right at Mere
traffic lights onto the A556. Then turn right at the next traffic lights into the
Swan's car park.

Swan Inn – 01565 830295 (Scottish & Newcastle)

The Swan's many extensions have turned it into a large residential estab-
lishment catering for many people staying in the area, either on business or
'en route' to Manchester Airport – perhaps to go on holiday. However, the
front of The Swan is the original building. Dating from the 17th century
when it was a busy coaching inn, the thickness of the outside walls are a
sure indication of age. Here, both Cavaliers and Roundheads sought sanctuary, at different times, during the Civil War, and Prince Rupert and his
army passed by on their great march north in 1644, to their defeat at Crom-
well's hands on Marston Moor in Yorkshire.

Walkers, dogs and ramblers are all welcome. A variety of beers are offered
including John Smiths. Bar snacks and a full restaurant menu are available
every day 12 noon-2.30pm and 6pm-9.30pm, and the bar is open all day.

The Walk

Leave the pub car park, cross the busy A556, and proceed past Bucklow Garage down Chapel Lane. You soon pass the United Reformed Church and
continue until, after passing a small wood, you turn right at a signpost,
down a grassy track. The rounded marks of horseshoes indent the grass as
you walk along the field's side to a thatched cottage. Then keep ahead to the
road.

Turn left past a still pond and Rushford Cottage, listening to the muted
murmur of distant traffic as you turn left at the next cottage, over a stile hidden by hawthorn. Then go diagonally right down to the valley floor, where
you cross two stiles before turning right to pass a wishing well in the next
small field. An attractive stile takes you to a farm track, which you cross,
then bear left to another stile into a field. Continue along the side of this,
parallel with the stream below, and keep ahead again at the end, passing a

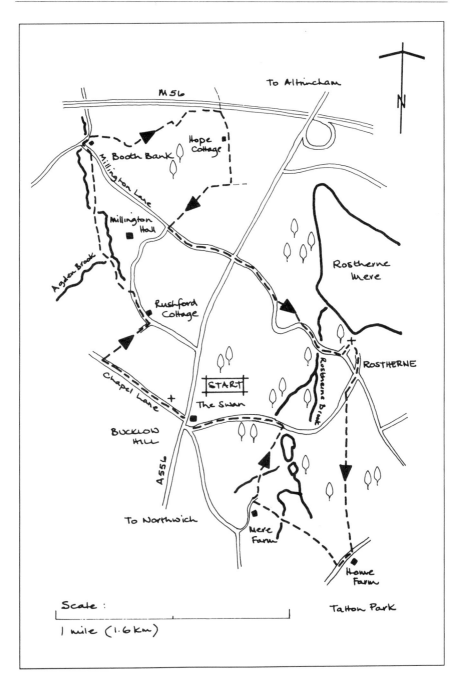

Scale :

1 mile (1.6 km)

gate on your right to go over a stile and cross another stream. After this, walk alongside a barbed wire fence, picking your way through bramble patches to a further stile, which takes you into a field.

Follow the line of oaks across this field, walking alongside the stream to a stile and a rough farm track. Cross this and stay beside the stream to the end of the field, where you bear right over it. The stone for Rostherne Church came from the quarry here, and its sand was of great value for road building. Bonny Prince Charlie is also reputed to have been turned back in this pretty valley, its wooded slopes a mass of bluebells. Continue up the hill for a little way, then go left over a stile into a meadow, where friendly horses may be grazing. Keep along the hillside here, parallel with the stream, until you reach a stile which takes you onto Millington Lane.

Turn left to Reddy Lane, named when sandstone grit, from the quarry, fell off the carts and was reddened by rain. Go right along here, and right again up a track beside Booth Bank Farm. (If you want to do an interesting detour, keep along Reddy Lane until, under the motorway, you will see a plaque where Booth Bank Methodist Chapel once stood. It also commemorates John Wesley's visits to the area, when he stayed at Old Booth Bank Farm and preached under the oak still standing in front of the house.)

Return to the track and continue up it until you go through a large gap in the hedge, and turn left along the field's side to a stile. Then keep ahead parallel with a wood to a further stile, where you turn left and then right, walking beside the hedge to a track. Turn right here, and cross two stiles as you pass Hope Cottage, thickly protected by its holly hedge. Then keep ahead over a field, going through a facing gate and then over a stile on your right. After this, crossing a further field, and walking alongside the hedge of another, will take you back to Millington Lane.

Turn left here to the A556 (once Watling Street – an ancient Roman road) which you cross, and continue down the road to Rostherne. Bear left at the footpath which runs alongside a wood and cuts off a bend. On your return to the road turn left to cross Rostherne Brook, as it gushes rapidly out of a wood and then courses more gently through meadowland to the mere. At the church's entrance turn left again to walk up through a lychgate. Dating from 1640, it is probably the oldest and most unusual gate in Cheshire, and the oldest lychgate in England. It closes automatically by means of a weighted cord passing over a high wheel.

St Mary's church, its tower housing six heavy bells, stands above the national nature reserve and bird sanctuary of Rostherne Mere – the largest natural lake in Cheshire and over 100 feet deep. Smelt, a small, salt-water fish which, like salmon, spawns in rivers, is one of the species to be found

Probably the oldest lychgate in England – at Rostherne

in it. Local legend says that on Easter Sunday a mermaid, whose home is in the mere, can be heard singing, and ringing a bell she has found on its bed.

After admiring the view, carry on up through the churchyard (dotted with tombs of the Egerton family of Tatton Park) and out through the top gate. You experience the village's rare and unspoilt charm as you continue past the old schoolhouse to the road, which you cross and walk ahead towards Bucklow Hill. Along here estate cottages, with pretty names and even prettier gardens, line the leafy lane down which you walk, before turning left down a track at the end of the first field. Keep down the side of the field here, then go through the kissing gate and make for the far corner of the wood over to your left, after which you cross over into the next field and follow a clear path between crops to Home Farm.

Turn right at the road here and walk past, first the farm then an old cottage dated 1626, before you turn right into the field. An ancient barn stands nearby as you follow the well-defined path, then go over or under the facing fence – depending on your size! Carry straight on towards aptly-named Mere Farm. Soughing trees form an attractive backdrop for the two meres, encircled by their fringe of riffling reeds. Cross over the stream and follow the 'rabbit track' over the next field, with Mere Farm on your left.

Then go through the gate onto the farm road, turning right along a pretty, hidden valley, an attractive waterfall cascading from its rocky lip. The footpath leads off to the left before the depot, and you go over the stile and over the stream. Then climb out of the valley and cross planks beside the gate into the next field. Follow orange bands on posts that lead over this field, before negotiating the stile into the next, and dropping down to the mere. There are even stepping stones over the marshy ground in this idyllic spot – fishing ground for Warrington Anglers. You then finish the walk by turning left along the winding country lane back to The Swan.

Styal

Route: Norcliffe Chapel – Styal Country Park – Oversley Bridge – Burleyhurst Lane – Ross Mere – Lindow Common – The Carrs – Twinnies Bridge – Quarry Bank Mill

Distance: 9 miles

Start: Ship Inn (SJ 839835)

By Car: From the centre of Wilmslow, head north on the Manchester Road (old A34), through traffic lights and straight ahead (second exit) at roundabout. Go uphill and take the first left onto Styal Road, signed "Styal". After just over one and a half miles, turn left into Altrincham Road. The Ship Inn is on the right and there is a small car park behind.

Ship Inn – 01625 523818

Despite its illustrious sign featuring a sailing ship this inn really got its name from the word 'shippon' – a place where muck was stored on a farm! In fact, it was one of five farms in the Styal area which at one time brewed beer, but was the only one to become a pub.

The Ship Inn at Styal – a popular pub for businessmen and locals

Terry Waite spent his boyhood in Acorn House opposite, which is now used by the National Trust. A photograph in the pub was taken only a fortnight before his abduction in Lebanon, and the locals speak of him with great affection. All were delighted in November 1991 when he was released after almost five years in captivity.

The Ship seems to bustle with activity no matter what time of day it is. The function room is often used for business meetings, and the pub is a favourite lunchtime haunt for those working nearby. Walkers too are welcome, and there is a family room for those with children.

Food is prepared on the premises, with a standard evening menu and, at lunchtime, homemade soup plus a selection of savoury dishes on view on the hot plate. These are specially prepared each day from a total of sixty recipes, and are served with fresh vegetables. The dishes may include pork chasseur, beef in beer, steak and kidney pie, and there are always quiches and salad for the weight conscious. A selection of sweets are also available, and my attention was drawn to Paris-Brest – a cream and choux pastry dessert shaped like a wheel, which commemorates a cycle race between the two French cities.

Drinks on offer include a Real Ale selection of Wilson's, Webster's, Theakstons bitter and Old Peculiar, together with Draught Fosters, Becks and Kronenberg. If you don't fancy beer, there is cider and an ever-increasing range of wines.

The Walk

Turn left out of the car park, then go right down Hollin Lane, walking past the simple stone war memorial. Turn right again down Holts Lane, passing mill workers' cottages with quaint porches and tall chimneys – a feature of the Styal estate. You soon enter Styal Country Park, owned since 1934 by the National Trust who succeeded four generations of the Greg family. The factory village was founded in 1784 by Samuel Greg, master cotton spinner. Here, water from the River Bollin could easily be converted to power the looms.

At the crossroads adjacent to the Apprentice House you can go ahead to visit the Mill but, for this walk, turn right towards the village. You soon reach Styal Cross, medieval in origin. Continue on to pass Norcliffe Unitarian Chapel. From here keep ahead again to the Northern Woods. One of Samuel's sons, Robert Hyde Greg, was a great collector of trees and shrubs, and many of the exotic rhododendrons, azaleas and conifers he planted still produce blazing displays of colour on these wooded slopes.

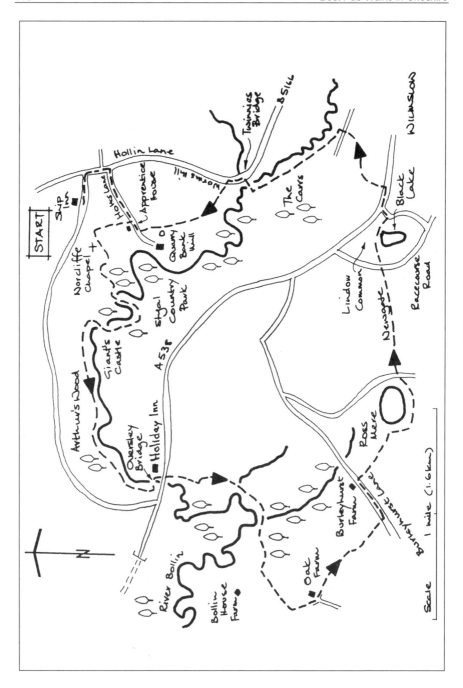

You can take either fork into the woods, but I think the left path probably takes you more directly down to the River Bollin. Continue right, following its tortuous course to a bridge, which you cross before turning left to climb high above the river. You then follow paths which all lead to a second bridge at the rock face known as the Giant's Castle. At its foot can be found the outlet of the tailrace tunnel from Styal Mill's water-wheel.

Cross this bridge and climb up steps, before dropping back down to the river, the slipping, sandy banks often reinforced by fencing. Continue through Arthur's Wood, and the noise of planes using Manchester Airport's runways over the A538 increases as you walk high above the river before turning left to cross Oversley Bridge and approach the Holiday Inn. Turn right down the side of the hotel car park and cut through a rough, overgrown area to a gap between the hedge and bridge railings.

Take care as you cross the A538. Walk a few yards to the left, then go through a metal kissing gate. Bear left to a second gate and climb steeply to a third gate. From here, cross a field (planted with maize in 2006, but with a clear path), then go over a stream and bear right at a signpost pointing to Castle Mill. Be sure to cross this field to the diagonally opposite corner, from where the path then drops through a wooded area to a bridge over a stream – a tributary of the Bollin.

Cross the bridge and continue through the wood with the Bollin below. After a few minutes, pass a three-pointer sgnpost with no names on its arms and continue through a muddy section and uphill to two stiles. Cross these then bear right (waymark) across a field to pass a small yellow marker post. Bear slightly right from here to a signpost pointing to Castle Mill & Morley Green, neither of which we want. Instead, cross the stile and turn left onto the tarmac lane. March along this, with Runway 2 to your right.

The lane soon turns left and you eventually reach Blakeley Lane and Oak Farm, where you turn left alongside farm buildings to a stile into a field. Walk along the side of this to a further stile and some ponds, and continue in the same direction to more stiles separated by a log bridge. Bear immediately right here, then continue in the same direction as before until you spot a stile in the hedge beside you. Cross this and turn right to Burleyhurst Lane, where you turn left.

At Burleyhurst Farm turn right, dropping down to a gate through a plantation of beech saplings. Cross the stile , and keep ahead on a raised grassy track. Shortly before reaching Rossmere, a lake formed some years ago by sand extraction and now used by the Prince Albert angling club, you turn right by an oak tree and walk up a cart-track. Before entering the next field, turn left at another oak and keep down the right side of a field. From here you have a lovely view over the lake – well stocked with roach, perch, carp, bream, tench and dace. A stile, tucked behind a holly bush in the corner, brings you onto a stony track where you turn left, still skirting the water. Keep ahead at a bridle-path junction which points right to Moor Lane and left to Morley, and look out for the stone statue of a gardener which stands in the grounds of Newgate Kennels. Then continue down Newgate to a road, where you cross onto Lindow Common. Go forward over this area, restored a few years ago as a nature reserve but originally bought for the town in 1897 from the de Trafford family. Black Lake provides seats and a pleasant picnic spot, and you finally exit onto Racecourse Road, turning left to the A538. ('Lindow' is thought to be derived from *Llyn dhu*, Celtic for 'Black Lake'.)

From here you turn right for a short distance, crossing this busy road as soon as you safely can. You then go through a gateway into a sports ground, where motor cycles and horses are prohibited. As you cross the grass, make for the far right-hand corner (behind the facing goalpost) where you will see a snicket. Go down this, passing the end of Park Road which is lined by pretty, terraced cottages. Then keep left where the path forks thrice, perhaps sharing the alleyway with squirrels and blackbirds.

Cross a road (Broad Walk) and continue forward between two houses before bearing left down the hillside into The Carrs – a pretty area of parkland, through which the Bollin meanders between grassy banks and the occasional sandstone cliff. The grass is kinder to the feet than the coarse gravel as you walk to a bridge. Then bear left where there are both toilets (open weekends only!) and a car park.

At Twinnies Bridge bear right at the information board, then climb over a stile on your left and walk across the field. Nowadays known as the Apprentice Walk, the youngsters working at Quarry Bank Mill walked to Wilmslow Church along here every Sunday. As the field rises to a stile the square cobbles show through, and birds are in abundance – finches, robins, thrushes – all adding joyously to the chorus. Keep ahead to pass the transmitting station on Worms Hill, then go through an iron kissing gate.

Cross the track to walk through the car park after passing the reservoir, where the water-wheel shaft may tempt you to visit Quarry Bank Mill below, with all its delights. Otherwise, to return to The Ship, continue along the path back to the village, and go ahead again at the next track to turn right past Oak Cottages. (It is worth wandering round the corner here to look in the window of the old village store. Further on, Oak Farm's black-and-white, half-timbered farmhouse is probably the oldest building in the village.) Walking along the cobbles to turn right at the road back to The Ship may prove painful, but it is worth looking at the village cottages, where the work of Michael Towey – master thatcher – is much in evidence.

The Pennines

Kettleshulme	Macclesfield & Alderley Edge SJ 87/97
Lamaload	Macclesfield & Alderley Edge SJ 87/97
Lyme Park	Stockport (South) SJ 88/98
Rainow	Macclesfield & Alderley Edge SJ 87/97
Shutlingsloe	Congleton SJ 86/96 and Macclesfield & Alderley Edge SJ 87/97
Wincle	Congleton SJ 86/96

Perhaps the Pennine hills that border Cheshire could best be described as exhilarating rather than spectacular, extensive views fanning out from them over bleak, sheep-strewn hillsides. Apart from the climb to Shutlingsloe's summit, and the short pull up to White Nancy, there are no other really breathless struggles, but it is an area where you can really explore the wilder reaches of the county. As an alternative to walking it is worth exploring Macclesfield's silk industry, or the estates of Lyme and Adlington – both connected with branches of the Legh family.

The Silk Industry of Macclesfield

The ancient town of Macclesfield grew up on the eastern edge of the Pennines, getting its nickname, Treacle Town, when a barrel of treacle fell off a cart and spilt all over the road. A visit to the Heritage Centre and Silk Museum gives an insight into the history of the town from Norman times. They are housed in a building dating from 1813, once a non-denominational Sunday School, where the children of working-class parents could learn to read and write. Nowadays, parties of school-children can take part in a one hour lesson in the Victorian schoolroom.

Heritage Centre and Silk Museum – Open every afternoon except Monday – Telephone: Macclesfield (01625) 613210.

The silk industry thrived in Macclesfield from 1743, with over 120 silk mills operating in the town by the 1950s, the last to close being the Paradise Mill in 1981, when the last handloom weaver retired. Silk trails can be followed through the town and the Paradise Mill, now a working silk museum, can also be visited.

Paradise Mill – Open every afternoon except Monday – Telephone: Macclesfield (01625) 618228.

Lyme Hall and Park

Acquired by the National Trust in 1947, this grand Georgian house has a collection of antique time-pieces, and there's a quiz to keep children busy while adults look round the spacious rooms in relative peace. The huge park, skirted on the Lyme Park Walk, has a large herd of red deer, a children's playground, a pitch and putt course, and bikes can be hired on which to explore its farthest corners.

To reach Lyme Park, take the A6 south-east from Stockport and turn right into the estate when you reach Disley. The house is open every afternoon except Monday between March and October. The park is open until dusk. Telephone: Disley (01663) 762023.

Adlington Hall

Built on the site of a hunting lodge in Macclesfield Forest, Adlington Hall has always been the home of the Legh family. The Tudor black and white building, built around a quadrangle, has the date 1581 carved above its entrance, possibly when rebuilding took place. Two massive oak trees still support the east end of the lofty Great Hall, which houses the largest 17th century organ in the country. While visiting, Handel may have composed 'The Harmonious Blacksmith' on it, and one can imagine the resounding notes from his well-known works echoing along the minstrel gallery, soaring through the rafters of the glorious hammer-beam roof, and on up the Elizabethan oak staircase, shivering the fir-coned newels on their way to the furthest reaches of the building.

The Rainow Walk passes above the Kerridge quarries from which the roofing slates came at a later date. The gardens were designed in the 18th century by Capability Brown, and in the grounds there is a fine yew walk, an avenue of limes, an ancient Temple to Diana, and a shell cottage. Although perhaps not one of the most magnificent stately homes of Cheshire, it has nevertheless played its part in much of the county's history, including occupation as a maternity home during the Second World War.

To reach Adlington Hall, take the A523 north from Macclesfield and turn left after about five miles. The hall and grounds are open certain afternoons between April and October. Telephone: Macclesfield (01625) 820201.

The Gritstone Trail

The Gritstone Trail is a 19-mile long-distance footpath down the westerly edge of the Pennines; it stretches from Lyme Park to Rushton Spencer, just over the Staffordshire border. As its name suggests, the Trail covers an area formed by millstone grit, a very hard form of sandstone. Ideal for the building of both roads and houses, extensive quarrying of this has taken place, particularly around Tegg's Nose.

Much of the route also follows ancient trails made by packhorses laden with salt from the Cheshire 'wiches', and cattle drovers travelling from Cheshire, or even Ireland, to Derbyshire and Yorkshire. Some of the walks in this book follow sections of the Gritstone Trail, and details are given of both prominent landmarks and pubs.

Leaving Lyme Park behind, the Bowstones are soon reached, followed by a steady climb to the summit of Sponds Hill. From here, the path drops down to Bollington, and a sharp ascent takes you to White Nancy, below which Redway Tavern and The Bull's Head offer welcome refreshment. From there, a breezy walk along the Saddle of Kerridge and on over moorland fields takes you to the Setter Dog.

A short distance away, Tegg's Nose affords spectacular views over man-made reservoirs, the ancient Forest of Macclesfield (the mill-and-market town), and the extensive Cheshire Plain. Ridgegate Reservoir basks in front of Leather's Smithy, and then the Trail continues, by-passing The Hanging Gate and Shutlingsloe's lofty peak.

The route then rises to the summit of Croker Hill before following the exhilarating ridge of Bosley and Wincle Minn. Here, the Queen's Arms (Bosley) to the east, and The Ship in the westerly Wincle direction, offer sustenance. Finally, the 'Gritstone' drops down through fields and woodland to follow the canal feeder to journey's end at The Knot in Rushton Spencer.

Kettleshulme

Route: Flatts Lane – Five Lane Ends – Saltersford Hall – A5002 – Charles Head Farm – Kettleshulme

Distance: 8 miles

Start: Bull's Head (SJ 989797)

By Car: Take the A5002 north-east from Macclesfield to Rainow. Then continue for four more moorland miles until you reach the Bul's Head in Kettleshulme village.

Bulls Head – 01663 733225 (Free House)

A listed building, the Bull's Head occupies one end of a terrace of stone cottages; its unpretentious exterior stands stolidly, fending off the biting wind which often swirls over these bleak Pennine slopes at the eastern extremity of Cheshire. It was once a coaching inn, and the older villagers can remember the stables standing at the back. In the 19th century a well-known Kettleshulme character with a beard seven-feet long, used to slake his thirst here and, lower down the valley, is a mill that once made wicks for candles.

The Bulls Head

Inside, the atmosphere is both warm and friendly, unspoilt by any fancy modernisation. The plaster and brick walls, adorned with gleaming brass platters, are topped by solid oak beams. The pub serves mainly hard-working locals and outdoor types, so no fancy drinks are on offer, but traditional Real Ale, including Boddingtons and various guest beers, with lager and cider as alternatives. Opening hours are Tuesday to Sunday, noon to 11pm (10.30pm on Sunday) and 5pm to 11pm on Monday.

Unfortunately, no food is available – it must be difficult to plan catering in a remote area where one never knows who might turn up, cyclists, ramblers, climbers, motorists out for a jaunt – or nobody if the weather is bad.Tea and coffee can be ordered and there's a pleasant beer garden at the back for warmer days.

The Walk

Walk up the hill, turning left and soon joining Flatts Lane where you go left again; then, before reaching a stream, turn right to Bent Hall Farm. Follow this track on to the next farm where you go over a stone stile to the left of the buildings and drop down to cross both stream and stile. Then walk up the hill, following a line of pylons and keeping alongside a hedge of pussy willow, holly and the inevitable hawthorn.

Continue to wind up the hill to the left of Clough Farm until you reach the road, where you turn right and then left over a stile. Cross a field here, which you leave via a stone step and boulder in the far corner. Keep ahead towards a house via a series of high stepladders and small gates.

On reaching a farm road you can, if you wish, make a worthwhile detour into Derbyshire for a superb view over the Goyt valley to Whaley Bridge, with the main Buxton road swinging its way along the valley side. To do this, turn left to pass Orchard Cottage and keep ahead across the field to a stile, then ahead again until the splendour of the view confronts you. Retrace your steps and continue down the road to Five Lane Ends (aptly named) from which you have a clear view of Windgather Rocks, where rock climbers may be swarming up the craggy faces.

At the road junction keep ahead down a No Through Road and, when you reach a cattle grid, cross it. Continue ahead again until you go through a gate and pass to the right of a house. Cross the brook here by means of a stone slab, then go through a gate and bear left to a stile. From here, keep alongside the stream until you cross this again and make for a substantial barn ahead, behind which lies another stile.

Continue forward again to a stile to the left of Green Stack, where geese may loudly object to your presence as you drop down to the farm road. Here you turn right to some flags, then veer left off the track, following the wall for a short way before crossing the marsh grass. Then keep slightly left to the stile raised above the top of the wall ahead, after which you cross a dilapidated stile before turning right along the road for a short distance.

Next, turn left over a stile by a gate, and continue down the track to Howlers Knowl. Go through the gate here and bear right past the buildings. Then exit through another gate, before turning immediately right through an opening to walk down the track to Saltersford Hall. It was built in 1595 by the Stopford family of Macclesfield and was then occupied by the Turner family. Richard Turner, who died at the age of sixty in 1748, was the first person to be buried in Jenkin's Chapel nearby.

As you cross a stile which brings you to the road this tiny bethel is hidden in a fold of moorland. It has stood on this bleak spot since 1733, when it was built using money donated by twenty-two local farmers. Always a meeting place for Saltersford's scattered community, there was a cross on the site long before the church, and a regular market was held there, when salt-carriers and cattle drovers would sell their wares. Jenkin himself was a drover and preacher who would address the country folk when business was done. It is to those men, forging their cross-country trails, that we owe the network of footpaths which traverse this area today.

Turn left and then right over a broken-down stile by a gate. Then continue down a grassy track and over a field dotted with molehills, walking parallel to the stream. Cross this at a bridge and turn right in front of a barn, where you negotiate a stile before following the stream again to a further stile. Here, the path has been diverted to the right of a house, so that you bear right over two log rafts, then keep ahead to the gate.

Turn left up the square cobblestones of the road here, and continue up a steep stony track until, at the end of a tree plantation, you go right over a stile and along a grassy track. Keep along the wall of this windswept, exposed field to a further stile, after which you turn left alongside the wall to a double stile. Then keep in the same direction for a short way until you bear right down to Moss Brook, which you follow through reed grass until you can cross it and go over another stile. Cross a tributary stream straightaway, then climb up to walk along the wall, squelching through marshy ground to two stiles. You can go over either of them and continue in the same direction as before down to the farm and then the main road.

Cross this with care, climbing over the stile ahead, then walking over the field to the farm road. Here you turn right, walking down a wet grassy area to cross babbling Black Brook before continuing up a sheltered valley path.

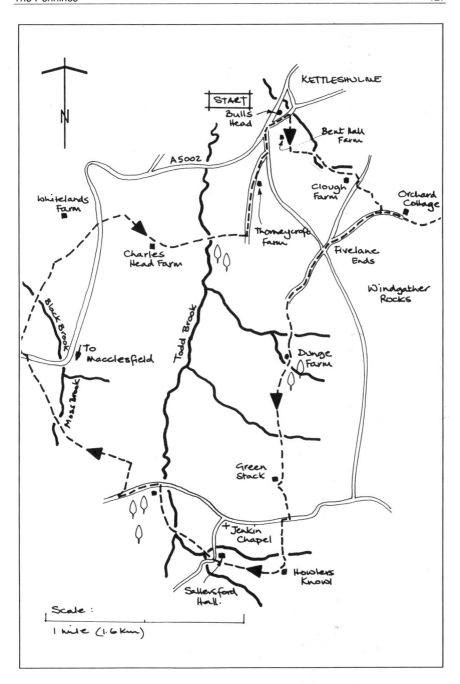

KETTLESHULME

START
Bulls
Head

Bent Hall
Farm

A5002

Clough
Farm

Orchard
Cottage

Whitelands
Farm

Thorneycroft
Farm

Fivelane
Ends

Charles
Head Farm

Windgather
Rocks

Black Brook

Todd Brook

To
Macclesfield

Dunge
Farm

Moss Brook

Green
Stack

+Jenkin
Chapel

Howlers
Knowl

Sattersford
Hall.

Scale :

1 mile (1·6 km)

N

After negotiating a stile turn right along a grassy track to a junction of ways, where you keep ahead through an avenue of stunted alder and hawthorn. Whitelands Farm stands high on the hill ahead, and the stream chatters away on your left until you eventually cross it and walk along the side of a field. Then drop down into shelter again to cross a stile and keep ahead to another stile and the road.

Cross this with care once more, and go up the stony track opposite. You can see the village of Kettleshulme tumbling over the windswept landscape as you cross the cattle grid and keep along this track to Charles Head Farm, where a black post box nestles in the wall – but not for your use! The farm-house dates from 1764 when it was built by a local man, Robert Pott. Inside is kept a leather-bound version of the Bible, known as the Charleshead Bible. Pass all the farm buildings before you bear right and left down a stone path to a stile; after which you drop into the valley past a lone barn. A foot-bridge crosses Todd Brook, and a worn-down grassy track takes you over marshy ground to a rusty farm gate.

Turn left along the farm track, passing Martin Stud dating from 1752, the date flanked by the builder's initials. Thorneycroft Farm is even older, dating from 1693. At the road turn left and then right back to the Bull's Head.

Lamaload

Route: Walker Barn – Lamaload Reservoir and Works – Snipe House – Hordern Farm – Gulshaw Hollow – Setter Dog

Distance: 4 miles

Start: The Setter Dog (SJ 956738) For ramblers who intend to visit the pub afterwards there is an ample car park opposite. For others a lay-by is conveniently situated higher up the road towards Buxton.)

By Car: Take the A537 Macclesfield to Buxton road which winds up into the remote landscape of the Pennine Hills. The Setter Dog is on a bad bend, the pub hidden away on the left, the barn and car park more obvious on the right.

Setter Dog – 01625 431444 (Free House)

Dating from 1740, the Setter Dog used to be the only pub in Britain also to function as a post office – the post box still is visible in the dark oak corner panelling of the tiny bar. The pub itself has had a variety of names, from the Dog and Partridge in the middle of the last century, to simply The Barn in more recent times. Its present unusual title, depicted on the inn sign as a silky haired red setter, is thought to have originated when a local man lost his dog in the surrounding hills.

'Snug' is the best word to describe the minuscule rooms where the solid stone walls and sturdy oak beams are all original, and the enormous gents (I write from hearsay!) was once a games room and card school for both local farmers and quarrymen. Both the bar, exuding a cheerful aura of friendliness, and the cosy restaurant, which once provided the licensee with his living quarters, have open fires, and children are welcome to eat in the restaurant with their parents.

The Setter Dog belonged to Smith's brewery before it was taken over by Marston's, though it is now a free house. There are three beer pumps to dispense two guest beers and, usually, Tetleys bitter.

The pub is open Tuesday to Saturday, 11.30am to 3pm and 5.30pm to 11.30pm, and Sunday noon to 10.30pm, serving food all day. Catering is described as being international but with an emphasis on English cuisine. As one replete diner commented, 'Not only is the food delicious but the quantity's exceedingly generous.'

Popular in summer, when crowds of tourists and ramblers sprawl on the sandstone walls and moorland grass of the tiny garden, in winter its patronage is sometimes increased because, during snowy weather, the Pennine road is often passable only as far as its door.

The Walk – In Winter

What better way to spend a cold December day, when frost spikes the grass underfoot, and the leaden sky glowers with snow-burdened clouds, than striding out over the hills. From the pub walk up the road towards Buxton until you reach the Peak National Park boundary stone. Climb over the stile behind this and follow the wall down the field, where bog grass stands stiff and tall in the wintry air and your breath billows ahead into the freezing sky. Keep above Vale Royal Farm, crossing a stile and then bearing right down the side of the hill and over the icy beck. Up the other side of the hill keep left along the wall and then right up to slippery stone steps over it.

The Peak National Park boundary marker – just up the road from the Setter Dog
(Photo: Graham Beech)

Follow the arrow over the next field, keeping between marker stones to further stone steps in the facing wall. The way is then ahead to the next stile and ahead again, sloping down to the right round the side of a hill. Climb over a fence and ditch, turn left across a field and cross a stony track, going forward to more stone steps. Plovers wheel and swoop as if relishing the arctic conditions, their shrill cries echoing non-musical accompaniment into the freezing air.

Drop down beside a wall to your right to more stone steps, stride across the ice-bound stream and follow a narrow path through reeds to a soft track by

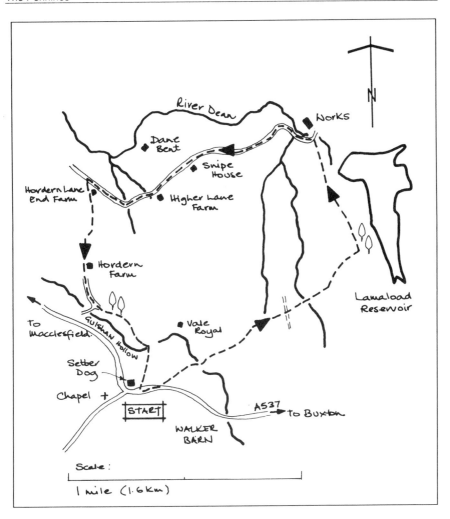

the wall. Here the track swings left at its highest point and you continue through a gateway down to facing trees and a stile by a gate. After turning left along the wall and climbing a stile, you ascend to a wooden post which indicates a viewing point over to Lamaload Reservoir. Drowning 42 acres of farmland, its sullen surface shivers under the lowering sky.

Descend from here to stone steps and cross the grassy track ahead to a plantation of triangular evergreens. As you drop down a steep slope, sheltered by wood and wall, gaunt branches of yellow larch, deprived of their brittle needles at the onset of winter, mingle with evergreen firs, still proudly displaying clustered prongs paired like ark-embarking animals on boughs stiff with silvery frost. Climb over a stile at the bottom, turn left at a signpost, and negotiate a further stone-based stile before bearing left again up the track and then right in front of a gate.

Continue down flags, by-passing the crystalline surface of a small, rime-covered pond, then bear left up the metalled road to Snipe House. In the valley lies Lamaload Treatment Works, opened in April 1965 by Viscount Leverhulme. Ahead a cattle grid straddles the road, rendered useless by the total disarray of adjacent walls. Mangers of hay provide welcome nourishment for the hardy sheep and, as you pass overhanging sycamore and oak, Dane Bent snuggly nestles into the valley below, while at Higher Lane Farm the road spans a stream plunging down its hidden bed.

After passing Hordern Lane End Farm, turn left over a stile. Then bear left up the steep hillside to a stile at the top, and continue with the wall on your right. Then negotiate a step stile surmounted by a sturdy log before turn left along a wall, and bear away up the field towards sycamores and another stile which takes you onto the farm track. A view of Rainow fans out gloriously below, enhanced by the rounded shape of Big Low and backed by an array of Bollington chimneys – relics of a bygone, industrial age.

Turn right along this track to Hordern Farm where you bear left at the end of buildings over stone steps, which take you to Gulshaw Hollow. Journey's end is in sight as you keep the wall on your left and stride along a grassy, frost-encrusted track, which leads over a frozen field to a right hand wall dropping down to a stile. Keep right past beeches silhouetted starkly against the cheerless skyline before following a wall and joining the track as it rises to the pub.

Perhaps the sun, a fiery ball, will leave you with a final memory as it drops down below the distant horizon of the westerly hillside, the sky briefly streaked with mauve and orange as darkness rapidly descends. If the walk has been really 'parky', with a near-arctic wind providing a good buffeting at every end and turn, you will be well ready to settle awhile before the Setter Dog's log fires, perhaps cradling a well-deserved pint of Real Ale while awaiting a steaming bowl of homemade soup.

Lyme Park

Route: Wood Lanes – Keepers Cottage – Bow Stones – East Lodge – Bollinhurst Reservoir – Elmerhurst Cottage – Throstlenest Farm – Maccles-field Canal – Adlington Basin

Start: Miners Arms (SJ 937818)

Distance: 10 miles

By Car: Take the A523 north from Macclesfield. Then take the next turn right after the one to Adlington. Keep left and right to Wood Lanes, where you turn left to the pub.

Miners Arms – 01625 872731 (Scottish & Newcastle)

Over 400 years old, the Miners Arms was once a farm, the bay-windowed section once being the shippon. Gradually, the farmer began to combine farming with serving ale to the local miners; eventually a licence was granted and the farm disappeared. Memories of the past are evoked in the spacious, one-roomed interior, with its exposed oak beams, magnificent carving of a miner's head, and a mural depicting pitmen hard at work on the coal face.

The pub is open seven days a week and serves food every day. Old favour-ites on the menu include chilli-con-carne, homemade chicken and mush-room pie and ploughman's. There is also a 'specials' board and bar snacks available. Outside there is a garden with a play area for children. Hikers are always welcome and Boddington's Real Ale is served.

The Walk

The walk starts with a gentle stroll down the track towards Lyme View Ma-rina, first crossing the railway bridge and bearing right over the canal. From this vantage point you can look down on Adlington Basin – a hive of boat-ing activity. Keep along the farm road here, edged by caravans, and then on to Lockgate Farm, where you keep ahead over two stiles. Then negotiate a further stile and turn right, to pass behind the farm veering left across a meadow rich with purple clover, bird's eye, milkmaids, buttercups and daisies. Continue up the hedge until you reach a track which leads to Shrigley Road, where you turn right.

At Cophurst Knott turn left up the bridleway to Birchencliff, passing a se-cluded and private fishing pool, where you negotiate steps jutting from a stone wall. Rabbits race around the terraced hillside, and lambs skitter in

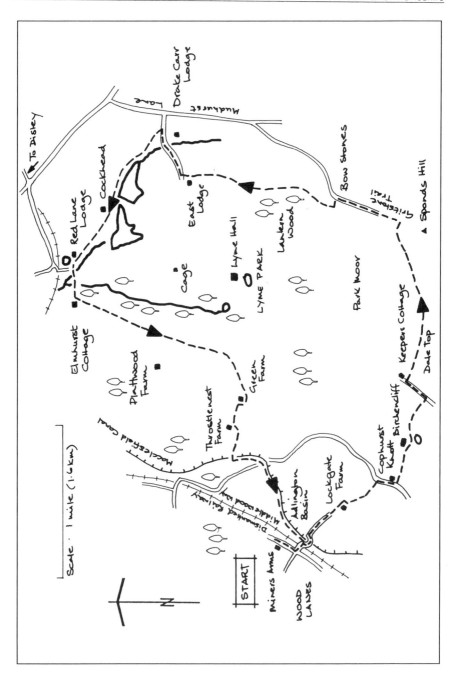

Scale · 1 mile (1·6 km)

START

N

WOOD LANES

Miners Arms

Middlewood Railway

Dismantled Railway

Macclesfield Canal

Adlington Basin

Lockgate Farm

Throstlenest Farm

Green Farm

Planthood Farm

Elmhurst Cottage

Red Lane Lodge

Cockhead

To Disley

Drake Carr Lodge

Moorside Lane

Mudhurst

East Lodge

Cage

Lyme Hall

LYME PARK

Lantern Wood

Bow Stones

Gritstone Trail

Spronds Hill

Park Wood

Keepers Cottage

Dale Top

Birkenscliff

Cophurst Knott

spring, as you continue on the track up the hillside, following the walls. Go through a gate and then turn left along stony Moorside Lane. Alderley Edge is clearly visible, stretched out above the plain.

Turn right before Keepers Cottage up a grassy track which forms the public footpath to the Bowstones and Kettleshulme. The Cage in Lyme Park is a significant landmark as you climb up the hill, scoured by disused quarries, clumps of wild rhododendron growing in startling profusion. After crossing the stile at the top drop down to walk alongside a wall. Over to your right is the trig point on Sponds Hill, but you keep along the wall to three mysterious pipes. Then continue to a signpost dedicated to John Lomas, where you turn left along the Gritstone Trail, revelling in the magnificent view into Derbyshire.

To the right of Bowstones Farm stand the ancient Bowstones, two shafts of late Saxon crosses, probably once acting as landmarks or boundary stones, as well as objects of devotion. The cross-heads which interface in the courtyard of Lyme Hall were probably once a part of these stones.

Turn left over a stile here, by a signpost donated by Davenport Townswomen's Guild in 1971. Then cross in front of the farm to climb a high stepladder stile and turn right along the wall, where Lyme Hall and its splendid park can be seen through the trees.

At the intersection of walls cross stone steps and keep left in the same direction down the wall, eventually crossing a little stile at the end of a wire fence. Then continue again until you leave the wall at the wood, turn right to cross a stream, then bear left to a bright green sign. To your left is East Lodge and a track to Lyme Hall, but you go right along a stony track flanked by an avenue of hawthorn, beech, elder, oak, ash and horse chestnut. Can you pick them all out – and perhaps others?

Where a road goes right to Drake Carr Cottage you turn left over a stile and, ignoring the path ahead, keep to the left of the wood down a grassy path. You soon continue alongside a wall which runs above the reservoir. In May, rhododendrons form a mass of colour on the far bank as you continue over a flat stone stile, to follow the wall and a fence to a further stile. Keep ahead here through Cockhead, then go ahead again through a steel gate, crossing a field to a stile where notices warn of dangerous, deep lagoons.

From here, keep ahead down a grassy track to the road, where you turn right to Red Lane Lodge. Then turn left, and go ahead at the crossroads along the Elmerhurst Trail, signposted Plattwood Farm. Cross the brook, continue up the stony track and over a step-ladder, then keep left in front of Elmerhurst Cottage. After this, you turn off the road, bear right up the hillside and go through a gate. Then turn left, walking parallel to the road at this higher level. After negotiating a stile, continue over the next field, mak-

The towpath approaching Adlington Basin *(photo: Graham Beech)*

ing for a hillside track adjacent to the wood ahead. Go through the gate out of the field and follow this track up the edge of the wood.

Continue in the same direction to a stone-step stile, the buildings of Plattwood Farm sheltering below as you pass a shed and trough, then climb over a stepladder stile onto a stony road. Cross this, then head off at an angle of 45 degrees right, over rough terrain, which takes you down to cross over a stream, then up the hillside to an indistinct green track. Turn right along this, dropping down to a high stepladder at the corner of Green Farm. Go right here over a low stile, then left past the buildings, before a right turn takes you back onto the track and down the hill.

You then turn left over a stile just before Throstlenest Farm, rounding the holly hedge and climbing over a second stile. Then drop down the meadow to a corner stile. Continue in the same direction to a stile on the right that leads to a stone canal bridge, its attractive iron interlaced railings providing safety as you walk over it and turn left along the canal bank back to Wood Lanes. If the pub is not open, tea rooms, a village store and an ice cream cabin all provide refreshments, and a wander round the plant nursery may provide you with a memento of your walk.

Rainow

Route: White Nancy – Saddle of Kerridge – Lidgett's Lane – Dane Bent – Lamaload Treatment Works – Ginclough – Oakenbank – Bollington

Distance: 7 miles

Start: Redway Tavern (SJ 937772)

By Car: Take the A5002 from Macclesfield towards Rainow. After crossing the Macclesfield Canal take the next turn left (in Higher Hurdsfield) to Kerridge and Bollington. Keep left along the hillside and turn right into the pub's car park on a hairpin bend at the far end.

Redway Tavern – 01625 573234/591 (Free House)

This country inn was once simply the end cottage in a row. In the 1920s the owner began to sell ale to the local quarrymen at weekends, and he also kept a smallholding behind the pub. At that time there were six quarries operating on Kerridge, and there were many part-time ale houses brewing their own beer and selling it to the local community.

When the Mad Major bought the cottage he persuaded the Goodwin brothers, who worked in George Unwin Hammond's Pit at Pott Shrigley and

The Redway Tavern at Bollington once supplied ale to the local quarrymen

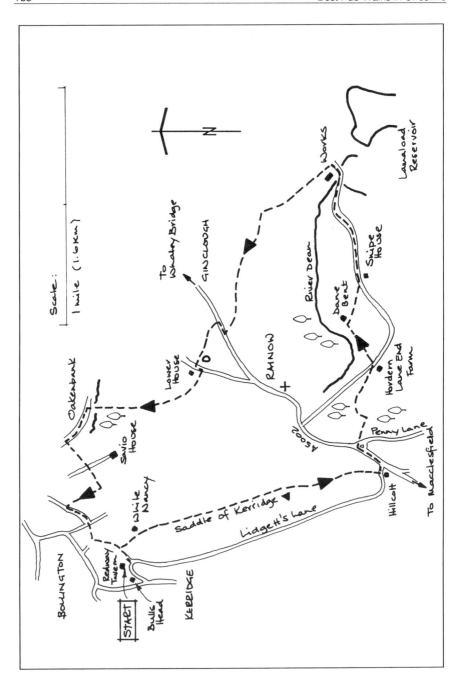

lived in the cottage next door, to sell. If you stand facing the pub you can see where it was once divided into two cottages, and inside an alcove remains where the Goodwin's outside door once stood. At that time the pub was known as the Mad Major, and pictures of the original building can be seen on the walls.

The Redway Tavern is particularly popular with ramblers walking the Gritstone Trail, and cyclists following the Cheshire Cycleway, and meals are served all day, every day. There is a special "Sunday brunch" especially for walkers from 10am, including free bucks fizz and free top ups to tea or coffee after purchasing the first. A children's room has been made with toys and games, and even goody bags to take away!

Friday and Saturday features "Dine & Dance", a 3-course meal and dancing until 1am.

Bulls Head (Robinson's)

If you only want a snack rather than a full meal, the Bulls Head lies just below the Redway Tavern. Once the magistrate's court for the area, it serves a tasty selection of sandwiches.

The Walk

Follow the footpath signposted up the hill from the car park. The view is magnificent as you climb higher, with Bollington (six miles in length) sprawling below. Many of the buildings are made of Kerridge sandstone, quarried from this very hill. Turn right off the track at the cattle grid and continue up the hill to White Nancy.

Long before White Nancy was built a beacon stood on the hill here (920 feet above sea level) where a fire could be lit to warn of invasion. The sugar loaf shape we see today was erected by the Gaskell family of nearby Ingersley Hall to commemorate the Battle of Waterloo which took place in 1815. It stands on the boundary of the parishes of Rainow and Bollington, and was built as a folly where people could picnic. To facilitate this, it once had a black, studded door made of iron, stone benches and a table – the slab top of the pedestal needing eight horses to drag it up the hill. The name White Nancy is supposed to appertain to one of the horses, and the structure was reduced to the stout white-walled structure we see today because of vandalism.

Do not cross the stile here, but walk along the brow of the hill until you cross a stile and a stepladder, then continue in the same direction as before. Cross the next stile at a tumbledown wall and continue up the hill and along to the Trig Point (313 metres, 1033 ft), from where the village of Rainow can now be seen sprawling on the valley sides. Almost under the hill lies a mill pool and chimney – relics from the last century, when 24 mills, all using water power, thrived in the Rainow area.

Marksend Quarry lies below as you cross a stile, then keep in the same direction between gorse bushes and climb over a further stile. Then you walk through an avenue of hawthorn trees to a kissing gate and continue down the hill to a beautifully-fashioned stile at Hillcott. From here walk down Lidgett's Lane and turn left at the main road.

You soon pass a garden sporting a signal box, and a station sign from Tunbridge Wells – owned by a railway enthusiast perhaps. It is difficult to associate the Rainow of today with textile works, coal mines, engineering and the production of steam rollers, all heavy industries effectively 'killed off' when both canal and railway by-passed the settlement.

As you reach the tiny triangle where Honeysuckle Cottage and Rose Cottage stand on the threshold of Penny Lane, cross over to the signpost indicating Macclesfield, Whaley Bridge and Buxton. Go through the gate at the left hand end of the terrace here, and walk up the field along a track for a short way. Then veer right to climb the hill, passing through three large gaps in the dry-stone walls. After the third, turn sharp left to steps in a wall, then veer diagonally right up the next field to more wall-steps that take you onto a track above a pine wood. Cross over, and clamber into the wood opposite, where a pretty path drops down through silent trees. When you reach a wall turn left down to a rickety stile and the road.

Turn right here and walk along the Water Board's road for a short way to Hordern Lane End Farm, where you descend wooden steps on your left. Then, after negotiating a stone stile, drop down the field ahead to a gate in the bottom right-hand corner. Cross the stream here as it drops down a spout, gushing to the River Dean. Then keep ahead to cross a second stream before walking along the track above the river to a stile fronting the farmhouse. Turn right up the farm track, passing Dane Bent – a typical, hard-working sheep farm where, in the spring, you may be lucky enough to see lambs born in the cosy shed.

Continue to a stile by a wooden gate, after which you climb diagonally up the field to Snipe House where, by the gate, jutting stone steps help you over the wall. Turn left over the cattle grid here and continue down the metalled road to Lamaload Treatment Works – opened on 21st April 1965 by Viscount Leverhulme.

As you reach the Works turn right just before the cattle grid, then go left over the River Dean and a stile. After this, keep ahead to a signpost, turning left to Yearnslow and Rainow. As you climb up the hillside, behind you Lamaload's massive dam comes into view. After crossing a stile in the wall, continue along the track as it veers left and splendid views open up over to Bollington, White Nancy and the Ridge of Kerridge. The stony track takes you past the turn to Cutlers Farm and Slack-oth Moor, and on down to the road.

Turn right here, along what was once a turnpike road into Derbyshire, then go left at the far end of a row of cottages. Here you descend steps to a grassy area, before turning left through a wall, then walking along Hayles Clough to a further stile. Cross over the stream here, and keep in the same direction alongside it to a step stile in the wall. You then go ahead again until you turn left along a stony track, passing a diminutive reservoir – perhaps once a mill pool – to a stile beside a dead tree. There are over 80 footpaths in the Parish of Rainow, many of them stemming from a time when people walked to work in Macclesfield or Bollington.

As you turn left down the road, notice how the nameplate of Lower House is ornamented with cart horse and plough – more normally used to decorate a weather vane. At the triangle turn right, and you have a fleeting glimpse of Rainow's modern housing development, discreetly hidden so as not to spoil the more attractive features of the landscape. Keep along the track of sand and stone, passing fields of cows in this more sheltered valley.

You eventually cross a babbling brook and wind round to the left past cottages. Then, when the road swings right, turn left over a stately stile of dressed stone, keeping ahead at further stiles to pass Ingersley Hall. Once the home of the Gaskell family, this Victorian building of blackened stone is now a Roman Catholic seminary, and has been renamed Savio House. Keep across the parkland surrounding it, crossing stiles at the estate road. Then drop down the next field, and turn right along a rabbit path parallel with the wood. Gaunt against the Bollington skyline stand tall industrial chimneys, relics from the 19th century when the cotton industry thrived hereabouts in thirteen mills.

At the beech copse you have to scramble down off the wall to the road, where you turn left past owl-topped pillars, then walk down a muddy path past an immaculate bowling green. Go slightly left when you meet the road here, then right, negotiating both steps and bank before you turn right again through a gate-gap. Keep round the side of the hill, passing dovecotes, their fan-tailed occupants cooing serenely, before bearing right between stone pillars. You then keep round the side of the hill again until you reach a road-end and turn left over a stile in the fence. Climb steeply up the hill here to the cart-track, where you turn right to return to Redway Tavern.

Shutlingsloe

Route: Clough Brook – Greenway Bridge – Hanging Gate – Macclesfield Forest – Shutlingsloe – Wildboarclough

Distance: 6.5 miles

Start: Crag Inn (SJ 982685)

By Car: Take the A54 north-east from Congleton, and stay on this road until you pass the Wild Boar, north of Wincle. Then take the next left turn, go right at the following junction, and the Crag is on the left after about a mile.

The Crag Inn – 01260 227239 (Free House)

Standing above flood level on the banks of Clough Brook, often simply called The Cragg, this remote yet spacious inn used to be a farm, part of the bar once the farmer's living room. As was often the case in these rural places, the owner began to brew his own beer for the local farmers, and nowadays the pub, with its antique furniture and open log fires, is well used by a variety of people, especially at weekends. It is an excellent stopping point for ramblers, although advanced warning of parties is helpful whenever possible. The police training school use it too, as a base for their outward bound courses, and its public telephone is a useful asset, especially in bad weather.

Don't visit on a Monday between October and Easter for it is closed then. Otherwise it is open for food and drink both at lunchtime and in the evening. The owner is also the chef, and his wife ably assists in the bar which serves, among other drinks, keg beer including Theakston's and Speckled Hen, a good selection of malt whiskies, or your choice from the wine list. If you are eating as well, there is a varied menu, the speciality being the Carvery, and a selection of homemade sweets. Children are allowed in the restaurant, in the sunny room upstairs with the lovely views, and the pleasant patio outside is well used on warmer days.

The Walk

Turn right as you leave the car park, then immediately right again up stone steps in the wall. Bear left up a grassy track, then continue to more stone steps in a wall. Cross the next field in the same direction to a further stile. Then keep ahead to yet more stone steps, and forward once more to a wooden stepladder. After this you walk beside the wall to another stepladder, then bear right to stepping-stones over the stream.

The imposing building at Wildboarclough was once the largest post office in England

From here, follow the line of telegraph poles to a gate, then go slightly right up the field to a track. (If there are cows and a bull in this field you may prefer to make straight for the track, where you turn left, rather than crossing the field!) Next, go over a stile beside a steel gate and turn immediately right, steps in the wall taking you onto a stony road. Keep left along this, passing above Lower Nabbs Farm, with its yappy, snappy little dogs, before the track drops down to the road and you turn right.

Continue to Greenway Bridge, where you turn right again over a wobbly stile and follow the stream. After crossing a further stile, and a stone spanning the water, wind to the left up the hillside, and you may well look in amazement at the multi-coloured rhododendrons thriving so well in this remote spot.

Do not cross the stream that tumbles down to your left but continue in the same direction, keeping to the right of a tumbledown wall. You eventually cross the stream below Oakenclough and keep on to the stile ahead. Then continue amid buttercup clumps to a small gate. Cross the track here and climb over the stile slightly to your right before continuing up the hill, with Shutlingsloe towering dominantly behind.

Cross another stile and keep ahead over a path of coarse grass, skirting two pools where plovers wheel and call. The huge TV aerial atop Croker Hill comes into view as you keep to the left of the wall, then turn right at the end through a gate-gap. Next, turn left over a stile and continue down a path through a gully to a stile. In front of you is the Hanging Gate with its novel inscription,

'This gate hangs here and troubles none, Refresh and pay, and travel on.'

And you may indeed be tempted to stop for refreshment. Dating back to the 17th century, and for a short time called Tommy Steele's, this pub has been a Free House for over 300 years. It is the start of an annual pub crawl known as the Sutton Eight, participants having a hearty breakfast here before patronising six more pubs 'en route' to Sutton Hall for an early evening meal.

To continue the walk, turn right along the road, picking out the saucer-shaped telescope of Jodrell Bank standing high above the plain. Then keep right at the next road as Teggs Nose rears above reservoirs tranquilly basking in sunshine below its forbidding bulk. (This may of course be a bit hopeful! It was originally written in the Summer of 1989 when the weather was superb!) The delightful country lane winds along past several old stone farmsteads before dropping down to the forest and bending right.

Here you turn right along the footpath to Shutlingsloe, which at first runs parallel with the road through the thick shade of Scots pine, before you

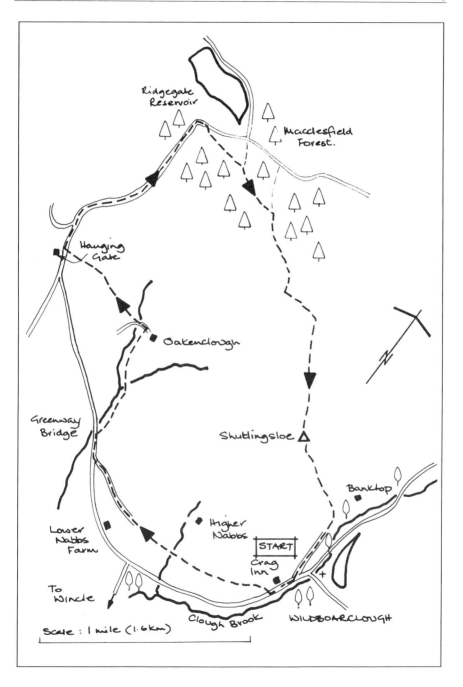

Ridgegate Reservoir

Macclesfield Forest.

Hanging Gate

Oakenclough

Greenway Bridge

Shutlingsloe △

Banktop

Lower Nabbs Farm

Higher Nabbs

START
Crag Inn

To Wincle

Clough Brook

WILDBOARCLOUGH

N

Scale : 1 mile (1.6km)

cross a plank bridge and then turn right up a pebbly track. Light filters through as you keep ahead along a grassy track, bordered by a broad-leaved avenue of sycamores. You then turn right again up another wide, well-used track, alongside which the pale, green-tipped branches of sitka spruce intermingle with saplings of sycamore and beech.

After turning right for the last time, the tree species become even more varied, sycamores mixing with silver birch, elder, rowan and beech, while shafts of sunlight dapple the path below. The trees soon open out to a perfect picnic spot amid scatterings of bluebells and bilberry clumps.

Take the right fork along here, climbing to a stile onto the moor, then continue towards Shutlingsloe. Wooden rafts placed over the peat preserve the path, save you from getting sodden feet and lead you to another stile. From here, go right along a stony path, negotiate a stepladder and then there is only the final scramble to Shutlingsloe's dramatic summit, 1659 feet high.

Approaching it from the back allows the view to appear as a total surprise – a rich reward for the climb. Steeper hills form a scenic backdrop to tree-encrusted fields that slope more gently down to the river. Wild boars may well once have roamed around the tiny hamlet of Wildboarclough. At one time it had the largest village post office in England; once a thriving carpet mill, the building is four storeys high, its front wall lined with twenty windows.

Your route off the hill is very visible as it drops steeply off the crag and, as the gradient eases, you bear right after climbing over a final stile. Turn right again along the farm road, the bluebell wood dropping steeply beside you, then a final right turn at the road will take you quickly back to The Crag.

Wincle

Route: Wincle – Whitelee Farm – Nettlebeds – Wild Boar – Hazels – Allmeadows Farm – Hog Clough

Distance: 8 miles

Start: Ship Inn

By Car: Take the A54 north-east from Congleton, and stay on this road until you turn right to Wincle. Ignore turns to right and left as you drop down into the village where the pub is on the left.

Ship Inn – 01260 227217 (Free House)

Alleged to be the oldest licensed premises in Cheshire, The Ship was originally a row of three, stone-built cottages; with walls three feet thick, part of the building dates from the 16th century. There even used to be a musket hanging on the wall, reputed to have been used in one of the Jacobite Rebellions, and, so the story goes, both innkeeper and customers were held to ransom in 1745 by a young man wielding it. Unfortunately, it was sold to

The Ship at Wincle may be the oldest pub in Cheshire

the Brocklehurst family, with other items, when one of the previous land-lords was hard up!

The Brocklehursts were the gentry and large landowners of the area, living at nearby Swythamley Hall just over the Staffordshire border. Sir Philip Brocklehurst sailed with Shackleton to the Antarctic in the Nimrod – the ship depicted on the inn sign. At one time the Brocklehursts had a small zoo on their estate from which some wallabies escaped and wild wallabies can still occasionally be seen roaming the local countryside.

The Ship is a Free House selling Boddingtons and interchangable guest beers. There is also a generous selection of wines, and food is served every day and every session except for Mondays when the pub is shut, unless it is a Bank holiday. Hot dishes include homemade steak and kidney pie, fresh trout from the nearby fish farm, fresh haddock and chips, and pâté. Extra 'special' dishes are added to the menu at weekends. In addition to a sepa-rate room accommodating ramblers and children (with their trappings or toys) there is a pleasant garden for use on warmer days.

The Walk

Walk down the hill from The Ship, turning right at the footpath sign before the first cottage. In summer cornflowers add delight as you drop down the steps and follow the path over a vertical stile, then continue along a field track. Turn right when you reach the rough, white road that takes you past the trout pool. Then, at the house, go over a footbridge to the left and keep along the footpath beside the river.

Bear right along the line of the fence in the next field, then follow the river over the following meadow. At the mill race do not turn left over the foot-bridge but go right to follow telegraph poles up alongside the wood. Then bear left at the footpath sign, up a mud track which takes you over a stile and into a field.

Continue up this field bearing right to a stile at the top, where you turn left along the farm track, walking away from Whitelee Farm. Bear right into a field where this ends, and keep ahead to a stile at the far end (near the left-hand fence). Then walk down a grassy track to the signpost ahead, which points right to Wincle Minn and left to Bosley Minn. (You are not walking either way, but the road that runs along the summit separating the two has seven gates that need opening – worth the effort for the magnificent views.)

Instead of turning left or right, go over a stile, to join the Gritstone Trail briefly. Bear right through an opening, passing a byre before keeping ahead

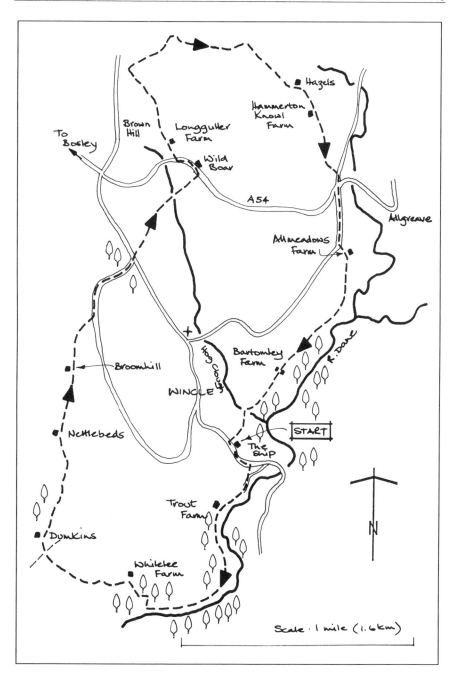

with the hedge on your right. Ignore the Gritstone Trail sign at the top (we leave it here) and keep ahead over a stile and up a grassy avenue, flanked by birch and hawthorn, to a farm track. Here, turn left through the steel gate and keep along the right-hand fence to a solid stile, after which you walk diagonally across the field, making for the corner where there is a gap in the line of oaks. Climb over the gate here and follow the fence down to Nettlebeds, then go through a gate and along a grassy track to the farm.

Turn right up through the farmyard, then bear left over the field to a steel gate in the fence. Do not go through this but turn right alongside the rickety fence to a stile at the end by a pond, then bear right through buttercups to a further stile. After bearing left past the farm, keep beside the hawthorn hedge to another stile. Continue in the same direction along the hedge for a short way, until you bear right across the field to a stone stile over the wall. This takes you down into the next field, which you cross diagonally (keeping right), until you reach a stile onto the road.

Turn left uphill to the main road, and climb over the stile opposite. Shutlingsloe and the Wild Boar pub come into view as you walk diagonally left across this field to stone steps in the wall. Then cross the next field in the same direction, dropping down the wall, before crossing to a path. Cross a minor stream here before you keep along the side of the hill and descend to the main stream and a wall. Rubber tubing allows you to cross the electric fence safely, and you bear slightly left to cross the stream with ease, before returning to the wall, then crossing the stile to the pub. This is the headquarters of the local clay pigeon club, and you may well have seen their discs littering the valley through which you have just walked. The Wild Boar is worth a lunch stop!

Take care as you leave the Wild Boar and turn right along the road, turning right again down the track to Longgutter Farm. From here, keep ahead over the gate and follow the hedge up the field, bearing right to where a stile hides in the corner. Next, keep the marsh grass on your right and the high ground to your left as you continue round the side of the hill – a veritable rabbit warren. Pass through the gate ahead before bearing left along the fence to a second gate, from which you drop down to the track and turn right along it.

Look out for the gravestone of Roy, a faithful friend, December 1923. Then carry on to Hazels, where you pass behind all the buildings and over the gate. Keep ahead through the next gateway before you drop down the field onto a rough track. Then continue through a further gateway, passing Hammerton Knowl Farm before meeting the rough road to it. After crossing this, aim for the stile in the fence ahead, then follow the wall on your left to a gate, where you turn left down deep tractor furrows to another gate and the road.

Turn right along the road and, at the crossroads, head for Wincle and Swythamley. You soon pass the wisteria-clad house of Longdale Farm and, at Allmeadows Farm, turn left down a footpath which takes you behind the buildings. Keep right over the grass to the gate, passing bushes of glorious broom in late spring, then continue down a track, formed of grass and stone, and flanked by wall and hillock.

Continue down the grass again to a narrow rabbit path along the side of the hill, where you take the right fork and stay high above the river; then a double stile leads to patches of gorse and bramble. As you walk along look out for a huge boulder on the skyline. Known locally as the Hanging Stone, it stands high on the Staffordshire hills. Keep alongside a wall, then pass through a gateway and cross a field to a stile, after which you keep along the valley side, in summer accompanied by swooping swallows, and bluebells and ferns share the steep drop to the stream below.

Eventually, you descend slightly to a stile at right angles to a gate, then bear left down a farm road, where a further stile stands in the wall. Walk over the field here, keeping the wall on your right until you go through a gap by an oak tree. Then, after dropping down to the water, a stile takes you into a bluebell wood and stepping stones cross the stream, after which you exit from the wood at spruce firs. Then keep ahead again (with a wall on your right) until you drop down left to a kissing gate, descend more steps to the road, and turn left back to The Ship.

South-East Cheshire

Astbury   Congleton SJ 86/96

Bosley Cloud   Congleton SJ 86/96

Marton   Congleton SJ 86/96

Redesmere   Macclesfield & Alderley Edge SJ 87/97

A variety of walking country is covered in this section of four walks. Wide views fan out over the Cheshire Plain from the summit of Bosley Cloud. Marton and Astbury are two quite different Cheshire villages – the former often winning the title of Best Kept Village (under 400 inhabitants), while Astbury's unusual church is fronted by a green, glorious with daffodils in spring. Redesmere completes the picture, its lake covering sixty acres, a habitat for a large collection of bird life.

The fertile pastures which cover much of the area are interspersed with villages, quiet market towns and country mansions. Here, inveterate visitors to stately homes, or walkers sated with fresh air and sunshine, or seeking to occupy that rainy day, are completely spoilt for choice.

Capesthorne Hall

Capesthorne Hall is the most northerly mansion. Situated opposite Redesmere on the A34, its facade is even longer than that of Buckingham Palace, and is topped by towers and turrets, domes and cupolas, while its southerly lawns sweep down to serene lakes spanned by graceful bridges. Tumuli in the grounds indicate activity in this area since prehistoric times, and certainly an earlier timber structure preceded the present hall – a brick column preserved on its site. Parts of today's building date from 1719, although the majestic centre part was redesigned by Anthony Salvin in the mid-1900s after a horrific fire.

Capesthorne has been the home of the Bromley-Davenports for many generations. They were originally chief foresters in the area, keeping law and order in the forests of Macclesfield and Leek. Later members of the family were Members of Parliament and even the Speaker in the House of Commons. Both Marton and Siddington are estate villages, justice at one time having been dispensed from the Davenport Arms (Marton) which takes its inn sign from the family crest of a felon, and this can also be seen on one of the houses in Marton village.

A great variety of sculptures, paintings and furniture are on view in the hall. In the grounds services are still held in the Georgian chapel, the warm colours of its interior enhanced by a painted fresco above the altar. The stable wing has been converted into a small theatre where productions are held during the summer months and, in the festive season, 'A Christmas Carol' put on by the family (with mince pies and mulled wine at the interval) is always a sell-out.

The attractive gardens are ablaze with colour throughout the summer, the glory of azaleas and rhododendrons followed by a variety of roses and other herbaceous plants. A herb garden and arboretum, a nature trail and children's adventure playground offer something for each member of the family. The grounds sweep down to artificial lakes built to enhance the vista from the house. You can spend time dawdling through Mill Wood, carpeted by snowdrops and bluebells, before returning to the house through lush meadows for an afternoon tea served in the garden restaurant.

Capesthorne is not open on Mondays and Fridays, but can be visited on all other afternoons during the height of the season, and at more selective times in April and September. Telephone: Chelford (01625) 861221/861779.

Gawsworth Hall

The ancient manor house of Gawsworth stands near the 15th century church of St James, in a village full of dignity and quiet charm. A house has stood on the site since Norman times, but most of today's building dates from the 15th century. Its external appearance is enhanced by the black-and-white of its timber frame, while inside are fine pictures, a rich collection of gleaming furniture, shapely sculptures and stained glass. A medieval tilting ground can still be seen in the grounds, and a tea room provides welcome sustenance.

Two widely different characters had their home at Gawsworth Hall: Mary Fitton, favourite maid of honour to Queen Elizabeth I, thought to have been the 'dark lady' mentioned in Shakespeare's sonnets, and Samuel 'Maggoty' Johnson, the last professional jester in England. He lies buried in the spinney known as Maggoty Johnson's Wood.

The days of clowning have long since gone, but today other forms of entertainment take place in the grounds of Gawsworth Hall. Several productions given by the Wilmslow Green Room Players take place in the open air theatre during the summer months. A Shakespeare play in June is followed by a Gilbert and Sullivan production in July.

To reach Gawsworth take the A536 from Macclesfield and follow the signs. Both house and grounds are open each afternoon between March and October. Telephone: Congleton (01260) 223456.

Little Moreton Hall

Two miles south-east of Astbury, on the A34, lies Little Moreton Hall. It dates from the 15th century and is considered to be the best example of a half-timbered, moated manor house in England. Built and owned by the Moreton family, wealthy landowners in the area, it was given to the National Trust in 1938 by Charles Thomas Abraham and his son, both distant members of the Moreton family and inheritors of the property.

What so impresses one about Little Moreton Hall is the building's perfection and lack of clutter. You can almost feel the atmosphere of bygone years exuding from its wonderful wooden structure and, for youngsters, there are all sorts of hidden passageways and secret 'bits and bobs'!

In the oldest part of the building children can search for the dog kennel and dovecotes built into the outside walls. The Great Hall is bare but for three objects: a great dining table, its surface fashioned out of one solid plank of oak; a cabinet housing pewter dishes found in the moat, one platter engraved with a wolf's head, (the Moreton family crest); and a spice cabinet divided up into tiny drawers and compartments.

The eastern wing houses the simple chapel, where a service is still held every Sunday, and an Elizabethan script of the Lord's Prayer can be found on the chancel's panelling. The south wing too is fascinating with its wainscoted long gallery – a place where ladies could walk in wet weather and children could race and riot in uninhibited fashion; a 17th century tennis ball was even found behind one of the oak panels.

The stable block and kitchens now form a tea-room. Outside, an artificial, grassy mound overlooks the immaculately preserved, formal 'knot' garden, where a perfect, symmetrical pattern is created by miniature box hedges and gravel, and the adjacent herb and flower gardens are full of plants discovered before the 16th century. As Charles Abraham, Bishop of Derby and donator of Little Moreton Hall to the National Trust, said on his first visit to the house:

'I shall not forget the thrill as I topped the rise after Scholar Green and saw the front of the old black-and-white house in spring sunshine, a rather wonderful shock of surprise and joy.'

Little Moreton Hall is open to the public every afternoon between April and September, and on weekend afternoons in March and October. Telephone: Congleton (01260) 272018.

Astbury

Route: Mow Lane – Fairfields – Congleton Golf Course – Astbury – Watery Lane – Lockett's Tenement

Distance: 5 miles

Start: The Horse Shoe (SJ 863601) (The Horse Shoe has only a small car park but there are two lay-bys nearby.)

By Car: Take the A34 south from Congleton. Turn left in Astbury. Then bear right on the outskirts of the village. Keep ahead on this road until you have to turn right at Whitehall. There is a parking place on the right down this road, and the pub is on the next corner.

The Horse Shoe – 01260 272205 (Robinson's)

This pub is hidden away in a small area known intriguingly as Lockett's Tenement; a previous landlord called Lockett is thought to have given the place its name. It has certainly been a thriving little community for many a year, and higher up Ganny Bank is the site of the old school and school house. The locals are sorry that another link with the past, the old-style phone box outside the pub, has been removed.

Up Ganny Bank lie mine workings where implements can still be seen lying in the derelict quarries. The conveyor belts used to run above the pub to the railway, where the cargo of lime was loaded onto trucks, and the remains of the stone supports, half concealed by ivy, can still be seen in a lay-by nearby.

One landlord of the Horse Shoe used to farm as well, and barns, stables and pigsties can still be seen. In fact, the pub used to be known locally as the 'Pig Pub'! At that time eggs were sold on the bar, and the patio outside was built on the site of the outside loo! The chimneys are original, but the brick walls, with their pebble-dash finish, were rebuilt last century, and glorious log fires burn brightly in the cosy interior.

Robinsons' Real Ale is sold – bitter, mild and lager – plus a goodly selection of bar meals. Savoury dishes include roast ham, Cumberland pork sausage, steak and mushroom pie, or something as simple as a Ploughman's. The selection of sweets incorporates raspberry and redcurrant pie with cream, chocolate nut sundae, and hot chocolate fudge cake. The food, which is all home-made, is served every day, and children's meals are also provided. Outside is a delightful grassy garden with swings, slides and a climbing frame – all conveniently situated adjacent to the patio, from which parents can watch their offspring play in safety.

The spire and towers of Astbury church dominate the village scene.

The Walk

Views spread out from Croker Hill to The Cloud at Bosley, and on to the Mow Cop ridge as you leave the pub car park, pass in front of the building and turn right up Mow Lane. As you climb Ganny Bank on the road to Biddulph and Mow Cop you pass a telegraph pole (on which a yellow notice proclaims 'COWS XING') and turn left up a No Through Road. Jodrell Bank rears up noticeably from the extensive plain below as you walk along the hillside before dropping down to a second farm.

Turn left here over a stile and cut across the field to the right of Fairfields, where you walk round the circular silage tank and cross a stile. Then walk behind the buildings to the farm road, turning right to The Homestead. At the country lane turn left over the railway, then go immediately right over a criss-cross stile of iron rungs and wooden supports. Walk over the field here parallel with the leylandii hedge and wriggle over a stile in the hawthorn hedge ahead. Then continue over a rough patch comprising nettles and thistles (a menace for those in shorts) to the edge of the golf course.

Follow the line of oaks on your left, which must once have formed part of a hedge, crossing the fairways with care until you reach a holly bush at the far side. Bear right round this to enter the safety of the wood under a beech tree. Then follow the path over a stream, and turn left below houses, keeping left again before climbing up to the canal. Cross the high bridge – no longer swinging – and drop into the wood, traversing it on the higher ground to another part of the golf course. (The next part is a mite difficult as the paths are obscure!)

You should aim to cross the golf course, passing a tee and a green on your right, before plunging once again into the safety of the wood. Do not go over the stream at the concrete bar but keep right along the path beside it through The Howty. After crossing two tiny tributaries you may have to scramble above a fallen tree, its branches fanning out over a large area. Then turn right and ascend a staircase which brings you back to the edge of the course. Wend your way along here, over rough ground, to a path where you turn left, and left again at a dirt road.

Continue down a pebbled path, through a new wooden gate and on down to the stream. After crossing this, and a stile, you turn right along the side of a field and, before long, pass a pond where a heron may be fishing. You soon reach farm buildings and an orchard, at the far corner of which you veer left over the field to a stile. Then climb up the field ahead and go through a grassy gap between houses (The Knoll and Potters Hill) before continuing down to the road, where you turn right.

You soon pass a rather grandiose schoolhouse and then the primary school,

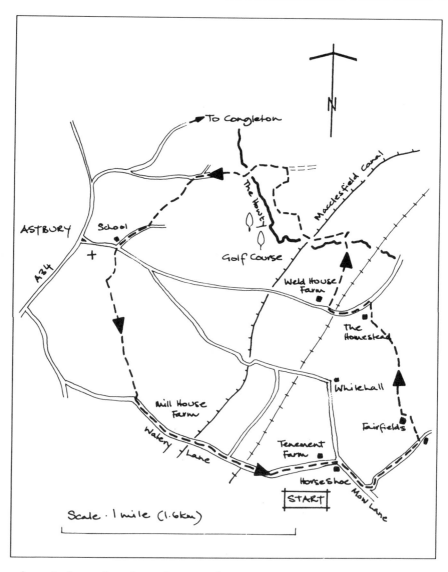

Scale · 1 mile (1.6km)

where Astbury church can be seen, dominating the village from its vantage point on the highest ground. The building itself is next in size to Chester Cathedral and Nantwich parish church. It is of an unusual design with one spire, and two towers adorned by grotesque gargoyles, their mouths wide enough for birds to nest in. In the churchyard is an ancient yew, reputed to be over 1,000 years old, its split trunk large enough to step through.

Fronting the church is a village green, its golden display of daffodils superb during the spring months.

Cross the road here and go down the public footpath to Watery Lane. Then, when you reach farm buildings, go through a gate into the field on your left, and make for the stile ahead. Here, turn left in the next field, go through the gap in the hedge and keep along the fence to another stile. Cross the following field aiming for the Old Man of Mow as he points an admonishing finger. This folly on the summit of Mow Cop (1,000 feet above sea level) was built as a summer-house in the middle of the 18th century. Mow Cop also witnessed the birth of Primitive Methodism in 1807.

You soon see a stile to negotiate. Then keep the hedge on your left as you drop down the next field, crossing the low fence at the bottom. After this, to reach Watery Lane you simply follow the cow path over the hill, cross a plank over the stream, and walk up to the five-barred gate.

Turn left along the road here and, after passing Mill House Farm, you soon walk through the echoing gloom of the aqueduct. Keep ahead at both turnings, which brings you to Tenement Farm (thought to have the oldest barn in Cheshire) before arriving back at the Horse Shoe.

Bosley Cloud

Route: Bosley – River Dane – Toft Green Cottage – Hillside Farm – The
Cloud – Gosberryhole Lane – Macclesfield Canal – Harris' Works

Distance: 9 miles

Start: Queen's Arms (SJ 919655)

By Car: Take the A54 from Congleton. Turn right at the traffic lights onto the
A523 towards Leek. After passing the church, the Queen's Arms is on the left
in Bosley village.

Queen's Arms – 01260 223267 (In Partnership)

Dating from the 17th century, this was once a coaching inn on the Macclesfield to Leek road, with stabling behind, and rooms where travellers could
spend the night. Nowadays, many people visit it for lunch or a quiet dinner
in the evening, and it is particularly popular with retired people as there is
no juke-box or rowdyism. The separate restaurant has 16 covers and is an
ideal venue for a small function, such as a christening or Silver Wedding.
The pub has also been hired on several occasions for wedding receptions
when it has obtained a special licence, and the whole pub has been used to
cater for the guests.

For many years Bosley sported a famous tug-of-war team, which even won
the British Championship in 1959 and 1960. No doubt the locals involved
often slaked their thirst at the Queen's Arms, where the beer is hand-drawn
Real Ale – Boddington's Best Bitter and guest beers during the summer
months. Nowadays, food is served in the bar every lunchtime and evening,
and the menu caters for everything from a cheese sandwich to a T-bone
steak. In addition to this, a traditional family lunch is served on Sundays,
with roast beef and Yorkshire pudding.

The Walk

Walk down the road towards Macclesfield, passing the old Church of England primary school with its mullioned windows, bell tower and clock. St.
Mary's church has a stone tower dating from the 15th century, but the rest
of the half-timbered building was destroyed by fire two centuries later and
was rebuilt in brick. The stone font was removed at that time to a local farm,
where it was used as a pig trough before being rescued and replaced in the
church.

Bear left along a path through the trees here, which takes you high above
the conduit linking Bosley Reservoir with the canal. Then continue down
the side of a field, the Cloud looming large ahead, the continual fizz and

Across the Cheshire Plain from Bosley Cloud. *(Photo: Cheshire Life)*

crackle of electricity pylons above. Drop down through kissing gates into a little valley, which takes you on down another field and under a railway bridge to Harris' works. From here, continue over Lymford Bridge, which spans the pretty River Dane. Rising on Axe Edge, it is the main tributary of the Weaver, joining it at Northwich after winding placidly through Congleton and Holmes Chapel.

Climb steadily up the country lane ahead, celandine and dog's mercury peeping from the grassy verges. Then take the first left turn down a No Through Road, turning right at Toft Green Cottage over a stile, and crossing the field to a stile in the left-hand corner. As you continue up the next field to a stile in the wall, smoke from a chimney of the tiny cottage may be drifting lazily across the valley. Turn left along the road to pass Hillside Farm – how much a part of the landscape these stone built farms are, sitting comfortably on the slopes. Then turn right onto National Trust property.

This path is not advisable for any but the most agile. It keeps right amid clumps of heather and bilberry; craggy outcrops jut out above, and you can trace the line of your walk so far. Where this path forks go left up the path of an old stream where a goodly scramble takes you to the trig point.

The sedate, advisable path turns right at the small lay-by further up the hill. From here you follow a rough road, then turn right again to ascend steps

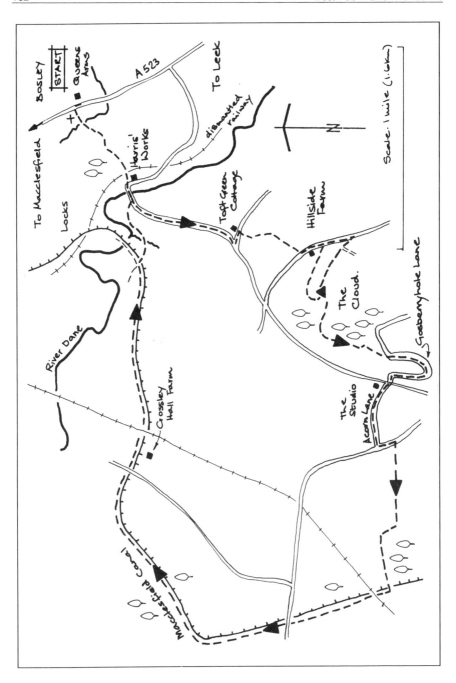

and walk up a gentle slope to the trig point. To the north, Congleton spreads out over the plain. Famous for the production of leather gloves since the 13th century, almost its whole population was wiped out by plague four centuries later. Sated with the tremendous view from the summit, continue along the path which goes behind rocks, then drops down and continues along the far side of the wood. When you reach a junction of paths turn right for more stunning views to south and west, and keep right along here to pass a sheltered pond with a variety of wild fowl. The stony cart track makes a large loop and, as you reach the road, you see that you have walked down Gosberryhole Lane.

Cross over the road here and continue past The Studio down muddy Acorn Lane. At another road turn left, passing houses before going right over a stile by a steel gate. Then continue down a grassy track until, where this ends, you bear right through a large gap into the next field. Keep ahead between two mounds here, before dropping down over a marshy area that is probably a dried-up stream. Next, you turn left, keeping away from the woodland as you cross to the far corner of this rough field, where smooth, grey-boled beeches line the valley sides, and past them is a footbridge over the canal.

Then turn right along the tow-path and walk under the railway. Sandstone milestones regularly indicate your progress between Marple and Hall Green as the canal makes an enormous loop following the land's contours. You might even rest awhile on seats provided for anglers from Stoke-on-Trent and, after passing under Bridge 61, ahead is Crossley Hall Farm.

After walking under the railway again, the twenty arches of North Rode Viaduct stand out high above the Dane's valley. Much of the stone for it was quarried from The Cloud, which also provided the foundations for many of the older Congleton properties.

Leave the canal immediately after Bridge 57 – before the aqueduct which takes the Macclesfield Canal high above the River Dane. Designed by Thomas Telford, this waterway has always been acknowledged as a great feat of engineering. To complete it over 2,000 men were employed, working a 50-hour week and earning just 2d per hour.

Walk over the canal bridge and cross a field, keeping away from the hedge and walking between gorse bushes on the higher land before dropping down to the fence ahead. The stile is to the left of the dip here – hidden in the corner. Your way then goes over the tributary stream, left over a stile, and alongside the River Dane to another stile into a large field. Make your way across this towards the Treatment Works, where you go through a gate and turn left back to the bridge. You then retrace your steps through the Works back to Bosley village and the Queen's Arms.

Marton

Route: Oak Lane – Marton Heath – Great Tidnock Farm – Higher Mutlow – Cockmoss Lane – A34 – Marton Church

Distance: 4.5 miles

Start: Davenport Arms (SJ 850682)

By Car: Take the A34 north from Congleton towards Alderley Edge and Wilmslow. After passing Marton Church, the Davenport Arms is on the left as you approach the village.

The Davenport Arms – 01260 224269 (Free House)

The unprepossessing exterior of this pub conceals a wealth of history. Dating from the 18th century, both it and the village form part of the Capesthorne estate, owned by the Bromley-Davenports. On the north side of the estate another Davenport Arms at Woodford is known locally as The Thieves Neck, and the inn signs on both pubs depict a felon with a noose around his neck. These derive from the time when the head of the Davenport family was also the chief forester who tried local criminals. He used to send his master sergeants out into the forests of Leek and Macclesfield to look for highwaymen, who were then tried and hung. In the licensee's living room above the pub is a small staged area where the trials took place, and it is thought that a gibbet was suspended outside from the opposite wall. (Beware if you have pesky children, although the present landlord seems benign!)

This room was also known as the sweating room, where tenants of the estate had to pay their half-yearly rent to the bailiffs. They were then allowed either a full meal downstairs or to drink as much beer as they could in the day. One tenant was reputed to have downed forty pints! He quoffed them free but pints in those days cost less than 1p – a far cry from today's prices! Another story is told of a customer deported to Australia, who became the first bricklayer to work in Melbourne.

The Davenport Arms was originally the village farm, the farmer starting to brew his own beer as a side-line until, eventually, the building became the village hostelry, with New House Farm opposite taking over the farming role. When the A34 was built there were drainage problems with surface water. Two underground tanks were constructed, one in the field opposite the church and the second in the pub garden. These successfully store any water that runs off the road.

Bar meals are served from an extensive menu and there's also a board giving dishes of the day. There is an extended restaurant which has an appetizing a-la-carte menu and the licensees, being caterers themselves are keen on this side of the business. Children, ramblers and parties are all welcome, and the garden offers a pleasant retreat in summer.

The Walk

Turn left as you leave the car park and then go right down Oak Lane, noticing thatched Pump Cottage, aptly named because the village pump still stands in front of it. Notice too the names down here – Oak View, Oak Cottage, Oak Farm. It is on the property of Oak Farm that the oldest and largest oak tree in England stands. If you look back as you come to the school in its sheltered dip, you can see it. Alas, the trunk is now split, but thirty years ago it measured 58 feet round its base.

Turn right into School Lane and keep along this country lane for just over half a mile, passing the entrance to Mere Barn, then Holly Bank Farm from where, in the distance, Jodrell Bank's giant radio telescopes stand out above the plain. It is easy to see how Yew Tree Cottage got its name, and soon afterwards you come to Pikelow Farm.

Take the next right turn after this, signposted to Marton Heath Cottage, passing the trout farm where two artificial lakes – Don's Pool and St Mary's Pool – afford excellent fishing. Continue to the wooded conservation area, where you may disturb squirrels and pheasants, before you pass Marton Heath Cottage to reach an area of marsh, the stagnant water silted by reeds, the banks strewn with creaking willows and vivid gorse.

Walk through the farmyard of Great Tidnock Farm, and continue in front of the farmhouse garden before turning right over a stile. Drop down the hill, then bear right, keeping the fence on your left all the way to the sturdy wooden footbridge over Chapel Brook.

Walk up the hill, to the right of more marsh, and turn right over a stile by a gate. Then continue along the field's grassy edge, bearing left up the hill to Higher Mutlow. Next, bear right through a kissing gate in front of the house, then left through another and along a track to the farm road. Before turning right along this, notice the remains of a huge chimney stack on the end wall of the farmhouse. Cross the cattle grid and take the second right turn, which soon brings you to the outbuildings of Mutlow Farm, which nestles snugly into the hillside, surrounded by a miscellany of animals. Geese, hens and ducks noisily revel in the duckpond's murky waters!

The curious shape of Marton's church tower comes into view along here, as

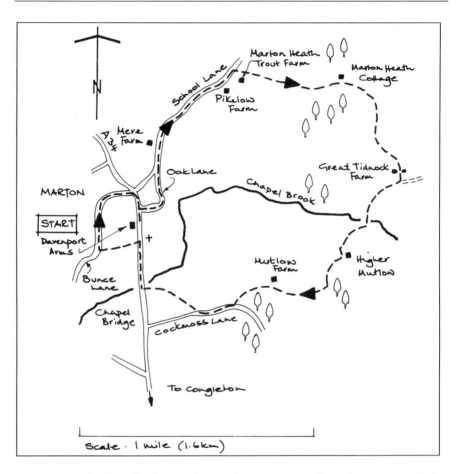

Scale · 1 mile (1.6km)

you turn right into Cockmoss Lane. As you pass a large house turn right over a stile to Marton, keeping across the field with the telegraph pole on your right, then walking alongside the hedge to stiles in the corner. Bear left to the gate, and right down a drive to the A34, where you turn right again, crossing Chapel Bridge as you walk to the church.

Marton Church

The ancient church of Marton is well worth a visit before you leave this little hamlet. It is the oldest half-timbered church in use in Europe, and is open every day until dusk. It was founded in 1343 by Sir John Davenport, whose effigy, and one of his sons, lie in the tower. The cross outside is even older than the church, and the roof slates came from the Kerridge quarries.

The footpath leads away from Marton Church – Europe's oldest half-timbered church still in use. *(Photo: Cheshire Life)*

There are touches of humour too to be gleaned from the church records. The south door was once given to a workman in lieu of payment and had to be retrieved at a later date, after it had become the front door of his cottage! Inside, there are two fonts. In Victorian days the simple stone pedestal was replaced by an ornate wooden one, which later became unfashionable, and the stone font had to be retrieved from a nearby farmyard!

As you walk down the nave look back at the ancient wall painting dating from the 14th century. It depicted the Last Judgment, and was touched up at some point, when one of the angels became curiously bearded! Further down the church the parish chest, which used to hold the ecclesiastical valuables, has six locks. The Vicar and churchwardens shared the keys between them, so they all had to be present whenever the chest was opened.

Having perhaps paused awhile at this unique little church, continue over the main road and the field opposite, where the path is clearly visible to the far hedge, after which you keep ahead to the stile in the corner. At Bunce Lane turn right, passing first an old, cruck-framed cottage, then Primrose Cottage – its garden brightly splashed with flowers.

As you reach the A34 look across at the house opposite (once the village post office), which still has the Davenport coat-of-arms high on its side wall. Then turn right back to the pub, thankful, as you pass the obsolete village pump, that the same cannot be said of the local hostelry. Its open fires, cosy, oak-beamed rooms, and nourishment 'par excellence', offer a welcome respite before the journey home.

Redesmere

Route: Fanshawe Lane – All Saints Church (Siddington) – A34 – Blake House Farm – Capesthorne Estate – Redesmere

Distance: 5 miles

Start: Large lay-by at Redesmere's southern end. (SJ849713)

By Car: Take the A537 west from Macclesfield towards Knutsford. Turn left (towards Congleton) onto the A34. After passing the entrance to Redesmere Sailing Club, take the next left turn towards Fanshawe, and park in the large lay-by at the south end of the lake.

The Walk

As you get out of the car, the vociferous clamour of many different bird species will greet you. Easy to spot are lapwing, pied wagtail, wren and chaffinch. Redwing and fieldfare are winter visitors, flying off to other climes before swallows, sand martins and house martins arrive for their summer sojourn. Besides these smaller birds, a large number of water-fowl are in noisy evidence. Moorhens scurry busily amongst geese and mallards, ruddy duck, tufted duck, pochard and coot (the dominant white stripe highlighting its black head from beak to forehead). Great crested grebe and golden eye may also be spotted if you're lucky.

At the western end of the car park turn left over a high stile by a steel gate, keeping a hedge, then a fence, on your right as you stay high above a recently dredged pond. Climb over a stile by the gate and bear left, passing the pond and making for another stile, ornamented by a bright yellow sign in the opposite hedge – not far from the left-hand corner. Cross the following field in the same direction until you see the chimneys of Simonswood Farm over the hill's brow. The exit gate is slightly to the right of these, and you then turn right along the road.

After passing Hall Farm you reach Golden Cross Farm where Ray Rush lives – known throughout Cheshire as the corn dolly man. The farm was the local pub many years ago, and a cosy room in one of the barns is his workroom, where he meticulously writes his articles about the countryside, and fashions his straw handiwork. He also keeps a small dairy herd of twenty cows, and all his farming is organic. Across at the farmhouse, nestling into the hillside, his wife offers farmhouse accommodation in this idyllic spot. They very kindly let people walk up through their garden to the church and, as you exit at the top, notice the stones which form the path and depict the Bible story from Good Friday to Easter Sunday.

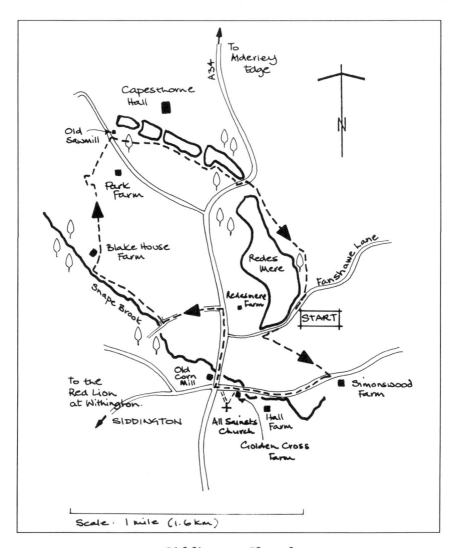

Scale. 1 mile (1.6 km)

Siddington Church

It is worth spending a little time exploring All Saints Church, Siddington,
'mellowing amidst fertile pastures at the foothills of the Pennines', as the
guidebook says. It has much intriguing history, and the little booklet about
it, devised by Ray Rush, is well worth the money. As you approach notice
the clearly defined bench mark low down in the wall – 326.45 feet above
sea level.

In the 19th century the weight of the roof was causing the wattle and daub walls supported by a timber frame to bulge out, so these were strengthened with brick, and the beams painted where the original ones still lie underneath. Inside, the rood screen may well have come from the nearby church of Marton when the Davenport family, taking up residence at Capesthorne, made Siddington their church. Attached to it, a cross of corn is surrounded by flying angels.

Over the churchyard wall the meadow, where cock fighting used to take place, slopes down to Snape Brook. You can imagine the spectators sprawled out on the tiered slopes of this natural amphitheatre. On the north side a mound of stones, resembling a heap of coal, lies on top of one of the graves. The man buried here worked at Crewe Railway Station for many years and his workmates wanted to erect a memorial to him. When, for some reason, their request was refused, the monument you see today appeared one night and has never been removed.

Exit down the church drive and turn left, looking over to a large, low area surrounded by sunken walls. This used to be a reservoir storing enough water to drive the corn-mill nearby. When you reach the A34 turn right to the building still called the Old Corn Mill, but now selling quality country clothing. You then cross Snape Brook, and pass Broad Oak Farm, then Fanshawe Lane, to the right.

Siddington Village Hall used to be the local school. Like many village schools it was forced to close in the 1970s when there were only seven pupils, who were transferred to the new Primary school at Marton. If you venture round the back you will discover the meticulously mown lawn of an attractive bowling green.

Continuing along the road, you soon reach a pair of thatched cottages, perhaps once a farm, and, opposite, Redesmere Farm – where various entrepreneurs sell kitchen crafts, furniture and signs. You turn left off the main road here, down a dirt track flanked by deep-set ponds. At a thatched cottage keep to its left, turning right at the back of a hut before you reach Snape Brook. Then walk by the side of a fenced field which borders the brook, following a path of soft earth. Geese flap about in the stream meandering below, and a fat partridge might flee from the hedge with loud objections.

Old oaks give way to mixed woodland of sleek, grey-trunked alder, birch and bracken. Tits twitter busily in the garden of a pretty thatched cottage, and you turn right in front of Blake House Farm. Where the track ends keep ahead down the left-hand field, turning left at the end before continuing into the next meadow. Then keep along the hedge on your left and cross a stile by a gate into a huge pasture, which you cross diagonally to the stile in

The bird life at Redesmere attracts many visitors

the far right-hand corner. Continue up the side of the next field to another stile, then pass the duckpond and cross this field diagonally, making for the lodge where there is a corner stile.

Cross the road and go down the track ahead, passing Dinghycraft and the Old Sawmill. Continue along the side of the wood, then make for the bridge over the artificial lakes. You do not cross this but go through a kissing gate to continue parallel with the water. After crossing a stile, bear left to the lakeside, then right beside a newish beech plantation to reach the A34.

Cross the road and then, slightly to your right, there is a gap in the fence, and a path down to Redesmere itself. Bear left to cross the overflow, then turn right along a stony track which leads to Redesmere Sailing Club. Bear left in front of the entrance gate, where boats lie askew on the grass, their masts clinking eerily in the wind.

Walk over the grass to a small gate into the wood, and follow posts along a well-drained stony path. After climbing over a criss-cross stile into a field, continue along the side of the wood to the next stile, then cross a hummocky field to Fanshawe Lane, where you turn right back to your car.

This is the only walk in the book that doesn't start from a pub, Siddington being one of the few 'dry' villages in England! However, the Red Lion in

Lower Withington is but a few minutes' drive away, and is well worth a visit.

To the Red Lion (Lower Withington)

Travelling south on the A34, turn right at Siddington church onto the B5392, and continue to the village of Lower Withington. Here, after passing the extensive village green – large enough for a football pitch – bear left onto Trap Street, where the Red Lion stands on the left.

Red Lion – 01477 571248 (Robinson's)

Built in 1896 by land workers using clay from the nearby fields, early landlords combined farming with the job of selling beer to the locals. Nowadays, this homely pub, selling Robinson's Real Ale, has the added attraction of being less than a mile from Jodrell Bank. Ramblers and children are always welcome, with tables outside for use in fine weather. There are also gardens, with swings and a tractor for the young and energetic. Advance notice is appreciated if parties or associations wish to visit so that the large room seating at least fifty can be made available.

Meals are served every day. The food is all home-made, with a huge range of 'specials' and all made from local produce.